I0429424

A Brief History of the Future

collected essays

Sunny Moraine

Other books by Sunny Moraine

Line and Orbit (with Lisa Soem)

Labyrinthian

Casting the Bones

Crowflight

Ravenfall

Rookwar

DEDICATION

For Sadie

Contents

On Play

On Tech

On Life

Acknowledgments

First and foremost, thanks are always due to Rob, who – for some reason – is still married to me after four years and shows no signs of giving up anytime soon. For putting up with my stress and my frequent moodiness, for wrangling me through five long years of a punishing PhD program, for providing various distractions, for propping me up when sliding into the fetal position and whimpering seemed like a fabulous idea, for reminding me that there's a great big world out there, and most of all, for loving me. Likewise, to the rest of my family, who may be praised or blamed for all of this depending on where you're coming from.

Heartfelt thanks are also due to the entire crew at *Cyborgology*: to Nathan Jurgenson, PJ Rey, Whitney Erin Boesel, Jenny Davis, David Banks, and Robin James, for helping me grow as a scholar and a writer in ways I never dreamed possible. Also to Jeremy Antley for pushing me to always think more theoretically, a project on which I continue to work.

Equally heartfelt thanks to everyone at Codex, without which and without whom I seriously doubt I would have come even half as far as I have regarding the business of wordsmithing.

To everyone at Darrow for being there, especially Ashley and Leah, because sometimes one kind of writing makes all others possible. Or at least massively easier.

And finally, to the Cat Cohort. You know who you are and you know why.

Foreword

This book came out of one of those *why not?* moments that occasionally strike us, where we're not so much looking for a reason to do something as we are for a reason to *not* do it. But in another sense this book is the product of years of fumbling. I'd love to be able to claim that everything in here is polished, complete, pristine and unassailable, but that would be a lie and not a very good one. This is a decidedly motley crew of content, drawn from approximately two years of two blogs: my authorial blog, and *Cyborgology*, where I write on matters sociological, technological, narratological, and various combinations thereof. All of that writing is part of a long conversation — or perhaps a series of conversations with a series of people.

It is not complete. It is not polished. It is most certainly not unassailable. Where appropriate, I've edited for clarity and for the sake of the change in medium, but for the most part I've left these essays materially unaltered. Transitioning a piece of writing from blog post-form to book chapter-form turns out to be a somewhat clumsy affair, primarily because of the problem of what to do with all the hyperlinks, but I've done what I can with endnotes, and I hope you might find them useful.

One of the things about which I've found myself writing repeatedly is the terrible idea that all the rough bits of our thinking should be done in private, with only the finished product displayed to the public. The core of that is something uglier: the idea that we should be constantly terrified of what we might do or say online, what information we might allow to leak out there, because it *never goes away* and because of course none of us will get jobs if anyone finds out that we drink on the weekends.

(Dude, none of us have jobs anyway.)

This isn't just about what we do or say online. I refer to this idea as "the tyranny of self-consistency", and tyranny is exactly what it is. None of us are neat, tidy creatures. We're all gross and wet inside. Frequently our thought processes are similar, and so it often is with every way in which we learn. Rather than keep up a facade that I'm very bad at, I've made it my business to be clumsy in the most public way possible, to grope forward where everyone can see, in the hope that a few of the right people might come over and help, or that I might be able to help someone else. Which is, of course, exactly what's happened, many times over. It's much better when we don't waste time pretending to be professional adults and instead just get on with our lives.

So, this book. It is what it is, fragmentary and odd, much like myself. The chapters are arranged not in chronological order but in a kind of topical flow that seemed to make some kind of sense at the time. This means that there are lots of internal references, but most of them are out of order. I worried about that for a bit. Then I decided that worrying wasn't helpful and went ahead and did it that way.

Are any of the essays any good? I think they are. I

definitely think at least a few of them are interesting. Are any of them useful? All I can say is that I've found them useful, as part of the clumsy process I mentioned above. So that's what this is, basically. A process. In a book. Which is, after all, what most books consist of.

Will you enjoy it? I very much hope that you will. Regardless, I thank you kindly for stopping by.

– Sunny Moraine, June 2014

On Writing

Cyborg Writing: Becoming the tools

(as Sarah Wanenchak)

> Life is elsewhere. Cross frontiers. Fly away. – Salman
> Rushdie, *The Ground Beneath Her Feet*

The patron of cyborg writing is the god Janus. Many-faced god, god of beginnings, passages, change and time as a stream through which we can freely move. God of transit, of transition. God of border-crossings. God of doorways. God of the spaces between.

In the beginning was the Word.

Well. Not literally. But you get the idea. Also, *literally* is sort of a problematic word in itself.

~

> Cyborg writing is about the power to survive, not on
> the basis of original innocence, but on the basis of
> seizing the tools to mark the world that marked them
> as other. – Donna Haraway, *A Cyborg Manifesto*

These words show up repeatedly in what I produce. There's a reason for that. *Creeds* are uncomfortable things

1

because dogma is dangerous, but creeds are also useful. Creeds solidify. Creeds brand, burn, scar. Creeds can also change.

~

"Every time we write, we become a cyborg and the more we use technology to write, the less aware of our enhancements we seem to be."[1] Except you and I both know this isn't entirely true, isn't the whole truth, because we don't *become* cyborgs, we *are* cyborgs, and writing makes us cyborgs in the same way that respiration makes us alive. Writing is how we know we are cyborgs. We write because we are cyborgs.

Cyborg writing is the first instant of picking up the tools. Cyborg writing is the process of making and unmaking and remaking the world in all of our own images. Cyborg writing is the internal made powerfully, dangerously, lethally external.

We have never "been aware of our enhancements". The instant we scratch words in the dust, the instant we *have* words to scratch, the world changes, and we don't see those changes, because we don't remember what it was like to *not* see them, to inhabit the world without words; we might as well attempt to imagine the universe prior to the birth of the current one.

We can try, mind. We just probably won't do a very good job.

A Brief History of the Future

When we imagine, when we see and hear and feel words inside of us, we run up against the barrier of our skulls and skin, the membrane that separates the *might be* from the *is*. Writing collapses the barrier. Writing is the breaking down of walls and the sundering of boundaries. When we speak of *enmeshing,* writing is the first act of the mesh.

~

I've said that keyboards gave me my words. This isn't exactly true either.

What keyboards did was bring down the wall; it was the collapsing of a dam and for the first time the words truly flowed into shapes cut into the fabric of everything, *look, look and see what I made.* I am with the words, I am the words, I make a space for myself outside myself and in that space I can *make* myself, I seize the tools, I have the power to decide what I'll be. When all you can see are words I am anything.

But I'm not a dog.

~

Once upon a time: Priests kept the books away from the common people, erected more walls even as they tore their own down. Then the printing press. Now the thing I'm typing on right now, making what you're reading, *hello.* Science, food production, medicine, communication, atomic bombs. Begin with writing. *This is where we are, who we are, who we'll be.* Not everyone gets to decide. The degree to which we are cyborgs is not evenly distributed. But the making and unmaking of the world is democratized. The process is slow. No one remembers what it looked like before it began. No one knows what it will look like when it's complete.

Complete may be a lie.

~

"We can communicate by voice without technology, but if we want to write something, we must pick up a tool in order to make that happen."[2]

Words were the first step; writing is the next. They're related, *enmeshed* if you like the term, but don't confuse one with the other.

Writing is the removal of story from past-laden oral history. Writing is the carving of the words into an eternal *now,* the projection of words into the future. At once writing removes words from time. They come from nowhere in particular; who knows where they ultimately go? They simply are. There is no direct dependence on others in the act of creation. A single writer picks up their tools. A single writer writes. For the moment the other voices are silent.

~

"When text performs a role, becoming an active agent in its own right, the process of reading adopts a conversational element."[3] Text gives writers agency. Through writing, writers *have* agency. Writers inhabit the text; the tools grant them entry. The dam comes down; we pour ourselves in and make a home there. Links are doorways to new rooms, to new homes. The words themselves only seize more agency in as much as the writer can act. The writer can reach out. Take your head gently in their hands. Direct your gaze.

"Hyperlinked texts present a cyborg face: they are there to be read, but they are also there to direct."[4] But the presented cyborg face is the face of the writer. It is also the face of the reader. The writer directs; the reader makes the choice to step through the doors. They choose to follow one path or another; to remain still. The writer and the reader become co-authors in the act of unfolding the world. Together they produce meaning; they reach through the growing holes in the wall and clasp hands.

Cyborg writing is telepathy.

~

I recently noticed additional crossover from reading practices on the Internet in a recent update to the book-reading software for iPads. The original version of this application was designed to carefully mimic traditional printed books, complete with realistic page-turning graphics, colors that replicate faded book paper, and digital bookmarks represented by red tabs flipped over the edge of a page. The new version added a continual-scrolling feature, allowing an entire book to be read as a single unending page, forever scrolling vertically. It seems, at least from Apple's perspective, that the single-page scenario of the Internet is perhaps preferable to the age-old feel of turning pages.[5]

Look: In my mind is a single flowing page, constant, unbroken; when I write it pours out of me. Not seamless but nearly so. It might be more seamless still, in time; there might be no more walls, just me and my words and the world. I reject the idea of "age-old". What age? How old? Better to ask what the words look like when still inside, how they flow outward, what they look like when they are at once inside me and inside you.

~

My cyborg writing is play, power, and connection. I'm reaching for you. Come *here,* I'll come *there,* and let's see what kinds of stories we'll be.

Fiction is Real and We Need to Use It

(as Sarah Wanenchak)

A great many words – though a lot of people would probably say not nearly enough – have been spent on the United States's drone war, on what it means, on who dies, on what it suggests about what war will look like in the future, though of course we appear to remain generally unconcerned about what it looks like to civilians on the ground watching their villages explode. But a recent piece by Adam Rothstein in The State[6] makes a powerful and provocative claim: That when we write and think and talk about "drones", we're really writing and thinking and talking about a thing that needs to be understood as distinct from the actual specific varieties of UAVs themselves. In fact, Rothstein argues, when we engage with the concept of a "drone" we have stepped from the realm of nonfiction into the realm of fiction:

> Drones are not real–they are a cultural characterization of many different things, compiled into a single concept. One writes non-fiction about the RQ-4 Global Hawk, the RQ-14 Dragon Eye, or the

iParrot Quadrocopter. These are all unmanned aerial vehicles, or UAVs, of which there are so many sizes, types, and ranges of purpose, as to make them impossible to conflate in a non-fiction manner. A iParrot quadrocopter has more to do with a model train than it does with a Global Hawk, and yet when we write about "drones" we are always referencing both of these together, and therefore, we are already out of the domain of non-fiction, even if we still surround ourselves in facts.

There are a number of points here that I want to address. First and foremost, the implications of what Rothstein is describing don't merely tell us a lot about how we think about drones and drone warfare; they also have a lot to tell us about how we experience and imagine reality itself. This is very heavy stuff already, but I think it's even heavier than it initially might appear.

In dealing with this first point, I actually need to proceed to the second one, which also amounts to a mild disagreement with/desire to expand on the characterization and terms of Rothstein's argument. I think Rothstein is exactly correct in pointing out that when we engage with different aspects of our world in different angles and with different elements of specificity and connotation, we often aren't engaging with them in ways that we would recognize as "nonfictional". That's all fine and good and true. The quibble I have – and it's at once minor and kind of important – is that Rothstein is still writing about fiction and nonfiction as if they were clearly distinct categories of understanding, though they overlap somewhat.

And I don't think they are. As least not so distinct as all that.

I've touched on this idea at a couple points[7] before,[8] and now I want to expand it somewhat.

Rothstein describes nonfiction as, among other things, a "historical project." In fairness he's mostly using the term in order to point out the ways in which nonfiction – to his thinking – isn't confined to "restricting itself to the face of a cultural characterization" in the way drone are. But the mention of history is significant whenever we end up talking about fiction and nonfiction.

Historiography is rife with a long and ongoing debate about the degree to which historians can speak with any objective accuracy about basically anything, or whether any historical project is necessarily going to be bent and biased by the historian's own assumptions, cultural and temporal context, mode of writing, narrative conventions, and a host of other problematizing things. That argument is a little beside the point for my purposes; what I want to use it to highlight is the fact that fiction and nonfiction aren't dichotomous binary categories but names for a porous and often nebulous reality of story and narrative and memory through which all of us move, and which all of us experience differently. This doesn't mean that nothing is knowable – not necessarily – but more that *it's just not that simple*. Fiction is characterized by invention born in imagination, but every time we open our mouths to talk about anything we're more or less embedded within that process.

There are elements of the created and elements of the "objectively true" in everything we talk about. In this sense, I think it's fair to draw a comparison between this kind of (what I'll call) *narratological dualism* and the concept of digital dualism.[9] Rather than distinct categories that don't intersect – you can be in one but not the other at any given time – I want to argue that we need to understand them as categories with different natures, uses, and intents that nonetheless constitute the same "reality", the same lived experience.

But also: discussions of fiction and nonfiction are not only marked by this kind of dualism but tend to privilege one over the other as more legitimate and real and – often – *good*. Fiction is regarded as wonderful by those who love it, but I think there's a general sense in our culture that as nice as it can be, it's just escapism in the end (especially what literary gatekeepers snootily refer to as *genre* fiction, best said with the nose uplifted and a faintly condescending smile) and ultimately kind of silly in comparison to the grounded and "real" work of nonfiction. The argument about fiction in historiography first really began when a bunch of historians in the nineteenth century started complaining that historical fiction – which was quite popular at the time – was muddying the waters of the discipline and degrading its truthtelling mission. What this argument really comes down to is whether or not fiction – or, in my characterization, fictional elements of understanding – can allow us to meaningfully engage with the truth of the past. Australian writer David Malouf argued that it could, and that in fact it was uniquely well-suited to do so:

> Our only way of grasping our history—and
> by history I really mean what has happened
> to us, and what determines what we are now
> and where we are now—the only way of
> really coming to terms with that is by
> people's entering into it in their imagination,
> not by the world of facts, but by being there.
> And the only thing really which puts you
> there in that kind of way is fiction. Poetry
> may do so, drama may do so, but it's mostly
> going to be fiction. It's when you have
> actually been there and become a character
> again in that world.[10]

This brings me to my final point: that fictive writing doesn't just allow us a deeper understanding of our past but a richer window into our present and a more vital imagining of our future. As I'll argue extensively to anyone who has the misfortune to raise the topic with me (I am so much fun at parties), far from being merely escapism, fiction – especially speculative fiction – is a fantastically useful arena in which to do social theory, yet it's one that most social scientists roundly ignore. Rothstein points out that science fiction is a perfect tool with which to allow us to engage with what we really understand by "drone" and what it can tell us about our general experience and construction of specific forms of technology:

> This is why we turn to science fiction to hear about drones–because this writing corresponds to our imaginary world, and the characterization we have formed around drones. We pull UAVs into our fantasies of the future and technology. To allow us a separate dimension of speculative investigation drawing upon the world of facts is science fiction's purpose, at which it excels.

Speculative fiction, among other genres, allows us to explore the full implications of our relationship with technology, of the arrangement of society, of who we are as human beings and who we might become as more-than-human creatures. It's useful not because it's expected to rigidly adhere to the plausible but *because it's liberated from doing exactly that*: it's free to take *what-if* as far as it can go. This differentiates it from futurism, which is bound far more to trying to Get It Right and therefore so often fails to do exactly that. William Gibson didn't set out to imagine right now, but he was able to get far closer to it than a lot of futurists precisely because he wasn't subjected to the pressure to do so. I think it was far more chance than any temporally piercing insight, but when we can imaginatively go anywhere, we usually get somewhere.

And then we can look back on what we imagined before, and it can tell us a great deal about how we got to where we are now and where we might go in the future – and where we *need* to go. We can't do pure nonfictive work on "drones", but to the extent that the work we do is fictive, and to the extent that we recognize this, it tells us so much in ways that other things can't and don't:

> The problem, is that in other less speculative forms of fiction that are more related to our present day emotions–like, to take one example, the novel–we are completely unwilling to engage with drones. We read and write in a world divorced from the spectacle of drones, and even more so, beyond reach of the fact of UAVs. The problem with fiction like *Zero Dark Thirty* is not simply that it is historically inaccurate. It is that it is alone in the field. War movies, terrorism TV series, and major news outlets have a monopoly on the characters of drones…There is barely any art and literature that attempts work with the more surreal aspects of our understanding of drones, let alone in a way that might connect our attention back to the facts of UAVs.

Fiction is part of what constitutes The Real. It's an investigative tool as useful as any other. We need to use it. But we can't do that until we understand it for what it is.

Sunny Moraine

No One Tells Stories Alone

(as Sarah Wanenchak)

It's worth noting that communal narratives – which we can understand as narratives that are constructed and related by multiple cooperating participants, sometimes in a hierarchical fashion and sometimes not – are by no means new. Narratives have always been communal to some degree, simply by virtue of the fact that no story, fictional or factual, exists in cultural isolation. Every story is embedded within a matrix of cultural values, assumptions, norms, etc. Fiction often draws upon influences of other fiction, sometimes merely in the form of homage and sometimes in adaptation. By the same token, when you tell a story to your friends about how you spent a weekend, that story exists within the context of shared culture, relationships, history on both a personal and a social level, and many other things besides.

Narratives can also be more literally communal. Many cultures feature storytelling traditions wherein the story is told through forms of call-and-response, with the audience just as much a participant than the official storyteller. Plays are arguably communal narratives; a play may issue from a single written source but every director and actor involved brings their own interpretation to the performance of the story, making each performance subtly – or extremely, in some cases – different. Gary Allen Fine has written extensively[11] on how tabletop role-playing games can be understood as communally constructed narratives of an excessively formal type. And in that same story about your weekend, your friends may interject with commentary or requests for more detail about certain elements.

So communal narratives are not new, in and of themselves. What is new, I want to argue, are the ways in which communal narratives are now being constructed and the spheres in which we find them.

Fiction

When we do talk about what ICTs have done to our narratives, I think we often neglect what we classically consider as "stories" – fictional narratives. But this kind of narrative is equally important to consider, especially given the ways in which our augmented fictional narratives are connected to fictional storytelling of the past.

One kind of augmented narrative with which I think most of us are familiar is, again, narrative constructed through digital role-playing. A lot has been written about

Second Life and *World of Warcraft*. Both of these examples are somewhat tired by this point but still worth mentioning given that they present very different kinds of role playing – *Second Life* is essentially goalless, with the emphasis on creativity, environment construction, and socializing. It could be argued that *World of Warcraft* is also goalless in the long run, as there is no singular "winstate" at which the game is completed; nevertheless, players are driven by the powerful immediate goals of leveling up and accumulating the best possible arms and armor.

Narrative also works differently in these games: in *Second Life*, the player has a tremendous amount of agency in the construction of their character's story, or freedom to actively construct no story to speak of (though simply by being in the game and interacting with others, a narrative still unfolds). In *World of Warcraft*, the game's larger narrative can easily be ignored in favor of stat grinding and item accumulation, but it's still there, and it subtly directs the background flow and logic of the game. Players still work within a narrative, even if they don't make it the center of their attention.

And there are other games where the construction of narrative is actually the primary focus of the game. "Pan-fandom" roleplaying games on the sites Livejournal and Dreamwidth[12] allow players to create journals for characters from various media and to "thread" those characters interacting with each other and working collectively to construct a larger storyline. Some of these interactions are plotted out before they are played, while some are constructed on the spot. But always the games are intensely narrative-focused and deeply communal.

It's also interesting to note that the actual structure of these websites affects the structure and logic of the interactions – the idea of the interactions being centered around turn-based threads within larger posts is entirely by virtue of how sites like Dreamwidth and Livejournal work. Because one might have multiple threads with multiple different characters taking place in a character's post, it's implicitly understood that all these threads are occurring concurrently, something that would be difficult to impossible to depict in a traditional singular-streamed fictional narrative.

This is actually a very important point: Storytelling is shaped, limited, and facilitated by the medium through which it is told, and digital media allow for – and force – particular kinds of stories to be constructed and told in particular ways. This is also not necessarily new; we can see it in older broadcast media, print media, and even board games.[13] What's important to attend to is how newer forms of technology affect how this happens. In Christopher Franklin's review of *Spec Ops: The Line*,[14] he notes that the actual structure of FPS gameplay encourages the narratives driving those games to adopt a black and white Manichean morality, where any action that allows the player to progress through the game is understood as unequivocally good, and anything that stands in the player's way is unequivocally bad.

In terms of a transition from older kinds of fictional narratives to newer forms, it's also worth tipping a hat to fanfiction. Fanfiction is often derided by many as silly, ridiculous, sex-obsessed, and of significantly lesser literary value than the sources from which it draws. Some of these things are true some of the time, but what the derision obscures are vital creative communities engaged in an ongoing process of complex interpretation, deconstruction, construction, and dialogue with elements of popular culture. These are stories that are created in an intensely communal process, often referring back to specific interpretations of the source material (called "fanon", in reference to "canon".

Fanfiction communities also aren't the only communities that engage in this kind of storytelling. Websites like Wattpad enable writers to construct stories serially,[15] developing them in dialogue with reader feedback. As Olivia Rosane notes in the article cited above, this goes directly against how most published stories are now written and delivered to the public, with all the messy creative and editing and marketing bits hidden behind a screen of polished packaging.

These kinds of narratives would probably exist without digital technology in some form; again, we tend to construct narratives communally anyway. But digital technology facilitates their construction, and affects what form they take.

Nonfiction

It goes pretty much without saying that things like the Facebook timeline[16] have a tremendous amount to do with how we construct – and display – our self-narrative. At the end of that post, Jenny Davis notes that "Through links and tags multiple narratives weave together to co-construct each others' stories and digitize an analog past." I want to build on that point, because I think it's important that we understand personal narratives mediated by digital technology to have a fundamentally performative nature.

This doesn't mean that those narratives are always either entirely public – or entirely private. It simply means that when we construct our self-narratives through digital media, we are engaged in an ongoing process of revealing and concealing, of showing some things to some people and hiding other things from others in a kind of digital Goffmanian dramaturgy. What kind of narrative we want to construct and display and how that's done is the product of interaction with others in different spaces; you may direct your self-narrative, but you don't construct it in isolation from others. Reality curation, as Jenny Davis has explained,[17] works in both directions. Further, as people comment on your posts and status updates, share links, and tag you in photos, they participate in the construction of your stories.

Additionally, as Whitney Erin Boesel described in her post on emotional self-quantification,[18] we construct deeper forms of meaning and self-knowledge through technology as part of our narratives - and these forms of knowledge may be shared with certain people and not with others, subtly affecting our own understanding and interpretation of that meaning.

Essentially, all narratives constructed through and mediated by technology are either implicitly or explicitly communal in nature. Again, this is true of narratives in general, but it's still important to pay attention to the *how* of that communal construction.

The end of narratological dualism?

I want to close by suggesting that something interesting may be increasingly possible – and necessary – concerning our augmented stories: the end not only of digital dualist thinking but of a kind of narratological dualism that draws sharp distinctions between fiction and nonfiction, and which privileges the latter as more legitimate and more meaningful. The Baudrillardian concept that it's now difficult to impossible to pin down an exact, objective, and original reality is, of course, not a new one, and I think that this "fuzziness" when it comes to the truth of meanings and events suggests some powerful things regarding how we understand fiction to be different from nonfiction. But what I think new kinds of storytelling also highlight is how deeply meaningful *all* forms of stories are to us. Fiction moves us just as powerfully – if not *more* powerfully – than many forms of nonfiction. Fictionalizing in the interest of eliciting emotion is an old technique: David Simon, creator of *The Wire,* has admitted[19] that relating factual accounts of Baltimore within a fictional frame very possibly makes people care more about issues of poverty, racism, and violence than would a strictly documentary approach.

Further, *our imaginations are real spaces,* just as the physical world is. We couldn't interpret anything that happens to us in the physical world without imagination on some level; it would be unnavigable. The "reality" of imagination is just as meaningful as the "reality" of the world that comes at us through our eyes and ears and skin, though that meaning might be of a different kind. In order to understand our stories and how they're changing, we need to understand that fiction and nonfiction are enmeshed, just as are the digital and the physical. And while we need to be sensitive to differences between the two, we can't privilege one over the other. To do so does a disservice to the richness and complexity of our stories.

Sunny Moraine

I Have Opinions: What's a writer?

I've been publishing science fiction and fantasy for almost half a decade now, but I still feel like I'm only just figuring out what the hell I'm doing. Therefore, it always makes me slightly uneasy to put myself in a position where I'm giving anyone else advice about writing and how to do it – both the mechanics and the practical elements – and even more uneasy when I'm talking about definitions of anything. And I'm sort of intrinsically uneasy with categories anyway. Given all of that, please let me go into this with the caveat that this is just my understanding of a thing, and it shouldn't supersede anyone else's understanding of a thing that may differ from my own.

All that said, I think "how do you know you're a writer" is a very interesting question to consider.

I'm not sure when I first started thinking of myself as a writer, but I know that I was long before I started getting stories published in places. What changed is that I started to be more *comfortable* calling myself a writer, and doing so in mixed company. What I wrote for a long time before original fiction was fanfiction, and I think most of us know and would agree that fanfiction is still verboten in many circles, and a thing to be looked down upon. And I don't think that's entirely fair.

I *do* think it's fair to call fanfiction a different *kind* of writing from original fiction in a number of fundamental ways. Those differences are subtle and not necessarily clear across the board – as with any system of categorization I think we need to leave room for a lot of boundary-shifting and liminal space – but I do think they're there.

Different is not *worse than.*

So what does a writer write? I'm pretty much with John Scalzi on this one:

> A writer…chooses written words, and chooses them not just for mechanical and practical reasons, but for (or also for) esthetic and artistic purposes. Writers *want* to write, rather than *have* to write. In presenting an idea, the medium they intend for it to be in is the written word.[20]

Intent is what matters here, to my mind. Not publishing – necessarily – and not whether you're writing with characters you made up. I think insisting anything else is categorical gatekeeping, and I'm not really a fan of that practice because it makes our collective world smaller and narrower, and therefore less fun. It also makes it more hierarchical. Hierarchy is generally bad.

So besides intent, what – in my estimation – makes

someone a writer? Here are a few things:

A writer writes. Doesn't talk about writing. Doesn't want to write (and stop there). A writer does the thing they're called, and does it with little fanfare, because it's the thing that they do. If necessary, a writer makes sacrifices in order to write. They make time. For a writer, the practice of writing is important enough that they organize at least a little portion of their life around making it possible to write. You have to do the thing that you're called. Otherwise I – and most other people, especially writers – don't buy it.

A writer *wants* to write, but is willing to write when they don't *want* to. This one is tricky, but I do think it's important. If writers are people who actually engage in the act of writing, then writers also recognize that any practice is work. It's craft. Simply waiting for the perfect moment when you feel ideally inspired doesn't cut it. If it really matters to you, it's something you'll carve out space for when you sort of don't feel like doing it today. That doesn't mean one can't and shouldn't take vacations from it, but it does – again – mean that it's important to have an explicit understanding that writing is work, and it's not always going to be a completely joyful, effortless experience. Along those lines:

A writer is constantly trying to be better at their thing. This doesn't mean beating yourself up for not working up to your own high standards, and it doesn't mean working to the point where you lose all joy in writing. It just means that – again – writing is important to a writer, and so is doing it well. Writing for the pleasure of it is an important thing – perhaps *the most* important thing – but anything that's worth doing is worth doing as well as you can, even if that ends up being not very well by most people's standards. A writer doesn't have to be a *good* writer to be a writer. But a writer should at least be interested in being the best writer they can be.

A writer reads. This may actually be the secret behind doing any of it well: if you want to write, you have to make time to experience the writing of others. You have to have interest in it as a craft outside of just what you produce, and that means reading and studying how others have done it. What to do, what to avoid. What you find important and what you think you can safely ignore. Styles and themes you may want to try and things that don't appeal to you as much. You can't pull this stuff out of nowhere. You have to go out there and learn. Reading is a never-ending master class. Take it.

So. I think that's what a writer is. And I think that someone who does all of those things consistently has a better than average shot at actually being a pretty decent writer, too. Going to go back to John Scalzi to close this thing out:

> You'll know when you're a good writer when your craft is good enough that you don't worry about whether you *can* do what you want to do with your writing, and instead you wonder about *how* you're going to do it. You probably won't notice the first time this happens. When you do notice it, it probably won't be a big deal. You'll be more focused on the writing.

Here's My Very Inspired and Productive Writing Process

I've talked a lot about my writing philosophy, and even some about how my personal stages of novel-writing work, but I'm not sure that I've really outlined the details of my particular process. So, to that end, here's how I usually do what I do.

1. Open up current project and stare at it for a while.
2. Wander off to mess around on [Tumblr/Facebook/Twitter/current pan-fandom RP game]
3. Go back to project and stare at it some more.
4. Write a few sentences. Maybe a paragraph or two.
5. Scroll back up to where I mentioned some esoteric detail that I need in order to continue but which of course I can't remember because I refuse to make in-depth notes on worldbuilding/plot/characterization because I'm not all that bright.
6. A few more sentences.
7. More staring.
8. Vanity Google search.
9. Become irritated with book blogs that refuse to give any space to my currently available books.
10. Do nails.

11. Sudden massive output that brings me up to about half of my minimum wordcount for the day.
12. Reward self with more messing around on [Tumblr/Facebook/Twitter/current pan-fandom RP game]
13. Check time and become anxious.
14. Frown at nothing in particular.
15. A few more sentences.
16. Jump at excuse to look something up.
17. Get distracted and stroll through Google.
18. Vanity Google search.
19. Drag self out of Google and back to project.
20. Make use of thing just looked up.
21. Worry about whether it's being used correctly and whether anyone will notice and/or care if it isn't.
22. Decide that probably no one will and even if they do I'm not all that sure that *I* care very much.
23. Check Amazon rankings for my currently available books because I refuse to internalize everything anyone has ever told me about how meaningless Amazon rankings are because, again, not that bright.
24. Check Goodreads reviews.
25. Become annoyed at Goodreads reviews that are stupid and written by people who are clearly correspondingly too stupid to appreciate my work.
26. Check [Tumblr/Facebook/Twitter/current pan-fandom RP game]
27. Vanity Google search.
28. Write a few more sentences.
29. Be struck by inspiration for a fantastic blog post. Spend about twenty minutes writing it.

30. Vanity Google search.

31. Check time again and become *very* anxious about how many other things need to get done today.

32. Tear through remaining wordcount.

33. Forget everything I've just written.

34. Reward self with lunch and/or [*Tomb Raider/Skyrim/Dishonored*/whatever other game has currently eaten my brain]

35. Spend rest of the afternoon on [*Tomb Raider/Skyrim/Dishonored*/whatever other game has currently eaten my brain]

36. Engage in period of self-hatred regarding everything that didn't get done today.

37. Repeat the next day, *ad infinitum*.

So that's it. It works fabulously. Truly it does.

Bird by Bird: The fine art of rewriting

I was having a conversation with some other writers on Twitter about the business of rewriting, and it came up that while there's initial drafting advice in spades, knowing how to rewrite seems to be a skill that's harder to come by. I said that I'm actually still afraid of it in a lot of respects, and I am – I just scrapped two novels (in fairness, I now think that was a necessary move in both cases) in order to start from scratch because working through it in a more piece-oriented way was too scary an idea.

But like all aspects of the craft, it's something at which I'm really trying to get better. So here, if it's at all helpful, are what I think are some good general tips for rewriting something.

(I should note that, like all writing advice, none of this will work for everyone all the time. Writing is such an individual activity – everyone has their own approach, and every project is at least slightly different, which means they have different requirements. So take or leave any of this as it's useful or not.)

So.

Write. Pretty basic, but sometimes surprisingly hard – I've heard others say and have experienced myself that fear of having to rewrite can actually keep one from writing at all. You can't edit something that doesn't exist. So you have to get that something out there on the table first.

Don't panic. Again, basic, but sometimes very hard. It's so easy to look at a writing project that needs a lot of work – especially something the length of a novel – and feel utterly overwhelmed. That's a natural way to feel, but it's also your enemy. Fear is the mindkiller. Along those lines:

Take it bird by bird. I keep name-dropping Anne Lamott and there's a reason for that: she's right about a *lot*. Here's one of my favorite passages from her, from which she draws the title of her "instructions on writing and life":

Thirty years ago my older brother, who was ten years old at the time, was trying to get a report written on birds that he'd had three months to write, which was due the next day. We were out at our family cabin in Bolinas, and he was at the kitchen table close to tears, surrounded by binder paper and pencils and unopened books about birds, immobilized by the hugeness of the task ahead. Then my father sat down beside him, put his arm around my brother's shoulder, and said, "Bird by bird, buddy. Just take it bird by bird."[21]

That said, don't be afraid to throw it all out. Because sometimes that really is necessary. Like I said, in the last year I had to confront that not one but *two* novels – novels that I loved, that I worked so hard on – just didn't work. As they were, they didn't do what they needed to do. Tweaking here and there wouldn't get the job done, at least not done enough. 90% of them needed to go. So I did that, and it turns out to have been the right move. That's rewriting so extensive that you actually end up circling back around to point #1, and I don't always recommend it, but sometimes it really is what needs to be done.

Don't get intimidated by structure. One of the things that makes rewriting so intimidating for me is that I don't think about plots in very structural ways. I usually work from only very rough outlines, and my plots develop organically. There's nothing at all wrong with that, if that's how you write best, but it does mean that the entire thing can end up feeling like a Jenga tower – you didn't go through with a very clear top-down sense of how it was all working, because you were immersed much more in the way a reader might be, so it can be scary to imagine pulling out the blocks and putting them in new places. But your book is not a Jenga tower. It's a book. No change you make is necessarily permanent. If you do something and it doesn't work, you can go back to an earlier version (provided you save multiple versions throughout the editing process, which you should *really* do). *You cannot destroy your book.* There is nothing you can possibly do to it that is irreparable. For all intents and purposes, though you can make detrimental changes, the thing itself is indestructible.

Solicit feedback and listen to it. That's not to say that you should always agree. I once walked away from a book contract because the changes that I was going to be required to make were not good changes and would not have made the book better. I have no doubt to this day that doing so was the right decision, though it was extremely hard. But if someone tells you something and you *do* disagree, take some very serious inventory regarding the source of your disagreement. Is it because you really believe it would be a bad change? Or is it because it would be a lot of work, or it bruises your ego? I have disregarded feedback for both (bad) reasons, and it's something I've had to learn to recognize in myself.

Don't put it off. This is a hugely important point for any large project. Because the longer you put off doing something, the more you forget what it actually looks like, and that's when it starts to take on monstrous proportions in your head. Your imagining of a project is *always* orders of magnitude more intimidating than it actually is. The more time away from it you spend, the more intimidating it will get, and the more you'll avoid it. Start editing early, and work at it consistently. Keep yourself familiar with your project. Keep yourself on task. But:

Give yourself a little distance. There should ideally be a break between the first and second drafts. I generally try to keep mine to at least a week. This is simply because by the time you're done with a big thing, you're too close to see it clearly. You need to come back to it with fresh eyes. This break period is also a good time to cast around for people you trust to give you feedback. Just don't let the break turn into avoidance.

Set deadlines and stick to them – which means don't come in too far under *or* too far over. This will help you with avoidance. It will also help you pace yourself and keep from feeling crushed under the weight of what you have to do. Give yourself enough time that you can work at it steadily a bit at a time rather than trying to tackle it all at once. I struggle with this, and with the ensuing burnout. Take it bird by bird.

Try to remember why you wanted to write it in the first place. There's nothing that kills enthusiasm for a project like a huge amount of time spent working on it. Again, this is true for so many things besides writing. I think everyone who writes a novel goes through at least a brief period where they just hate the thing. In the rewriting phase, try to find the things you love, not just the things that need work. Focus on the elements of it that are strong, and build the edits around that. Take pleasure in what you've created, and in how much better you can make it.

I think this last is probably the most important. Inspiration is *never* something on which you should depend in order to complete something the size of a novel, but the love of what you're doing that accompanies inspiration can be a powerful motivator, and it can carry you through hard times. In fact, in my experience, loving a book is sort of like loving a person. There's the first flush of infatuation, where everything is intense and wonderful. Then things cool off, and you really get to know them, which involves seeing their flaws and the less than lovely things about them, but which also gives you a deeper appreciation for everything you loved about them in the first place, and often reveals new and beautiful aspects of who they are as people. If all goes well, if you're really a good match, you love the person and then you *love* the person. I usually find that getting to the end of a book is the same. I may be impatient, frustrated, infuriated, and we might have to have some difficult conversations. We may fight. But at the end of it, I really love it, and I know it so well. That love can carry you through a relationship, and it can carry you through a book.

Be kind to your book. Be kind to you. Go and write.

OMG NOT ROBOTS: Literary fiction's technological tantrum

(as Sarah Wanenchak)

The way fiction deals with technology – the kinds of technology it tackles and how, and whether it actually *should*, directly – seems to still be a pretty thorny issue for a lot of folks. Or at least for some folks. Usually in conjunction with this is some variety of handwringing over what technology has Done To Reading, or Done To The Novel, often with the implication that no one reads anymore because ebooks don't count as reading and also everyone is too stupid and/or distracted to read anyway.

This summary isn't actually all that hyperbolic. Hang around a bunch of writers for long enough and you'll probably hear some version of it.

A less hyperbolic – though more biting – and more in-depth summary can be found in Sam Byers's excellent essay series on technology and fiction[22] in, as some perceive it, a crisis state (I really recommend it, it's both brilliant and infuriating). Novelists, it seems, aren't entirely sure what the hell to *do* with technology. What to make of it and what it means for literature, what it means for how their work is consumed, and most of all, how to incorporate it into the stories they tell. These are all reasonable questions to ask, potentially even questions that might lead to productive conversations, but rather than have these conversations, writers – at least the writers Byers is writing about – seem content to kick their feet on the floor and insist that it's just *too hard* and *who would want to write about texting and email anyway because it's so boring.*

No, seriously. Just listen to Toby Litt:

> I don't think I am alone in already being weary of characters who make their great discoveries whilst sitting in front of a computer screen. If for example a character, by diligent online research and persistent emailing, finds out one day – after a ping in their inbox – who their father really is, isn't that a story hardly worth telling? Watching someone at a computer is dull. Watching someone play even the most exciting computer game is dull. You, reading this now, are not something any writer would want to write about for more than a sentence.[23]

Just a side note? As a writer to my fellow writers? If you can't write something interesting about an "average" person doing "average" things in an "average" day, *you are bad at your job.*

Byers effectively skewers this claim by providing some great examples in which technology might not only accent but drive the action in a plot in some pretty compelling ways. As both he and Am Sonntag note,[24] this kind of thinking is also classic digital-dualist thinking: if technology is separate from "real" lived experience, why should one assume there was much to be gotten out of writing about it?

But then Byers goes on to ask a central question: *Why do many of the creators of fiction seem so frightened by technology? Why is it always The End Of The Novel when something new comes along that has to be incorporated into daily lived experience?* For, as he points out, this isn't even the first time this kind of panic has happened:

> Novelists are very worried about the novel. The novel, you see, keeps dying. No one thought much of it when it arrived; it had a brief reign as a fancy-pants new medium of entertainment; and then it just started dying all over the place. It became too popular. It became too cheap. It got a bit up itself and was no longer popular enough. It became elitist; then populist again. Cinema did for it. Television did for cinema and so double-did for the novel. Then the web came along and did for everything.

I'd like to offer an explanation, actually, one that I think Byers is by and large neglecting. There's something that he does – or rather doesn't do – through the series, that I've also purposefully done so far in this piece in order to emphasize it.

He doesn't talk about science fiction. Neither do any of the writers he quotes. It's just not on their radar. For them, "novel" does not appear to include "novel about robots".

So now we have to talk about Genre Wars.

It's probably a misnomer to call it a "war", but I enjoy the term. What it amounts to is a kind of aggressive gatekeeping, a long-standing defense of literary borders. *Literary* fiction – for best effect, tilt your nose slightly into the air and sniff when you say *literary* – plumbs the depths of the human soul, lays bare the hard beauty of human experience, because it's about *humans*. Not aliens, not robots, not spaceships. It's not escapist and childish. It's *real*, more *real* than SF could ever be. *Sniff.*

This is irritating, and has a lot of troubling cultural effects, but one of the ways in which I'd argue it hurts *literary* fiction (I'm sorry, I have a very hard time even taking that label seriously anymore) is that literary fiction has felt free to entirely ignore SF and what it does for most of SF's existence, with the exception of a few incursions like Margaret Atwood and – more recently – William Gibson. And when those writers and their work are accepted – even reluctantly – they're not SFnal anymore.

But the thing about telling stories with technology is that SF has always done it. We're not threatened by it. We know how to do it, and do it well. We have the tools that literary fiction needs, the tools without which they're panicked and grumpy. But they don't really *see* us, most of them. Or refuse to take us seriously. Protecting borders is still more important than facilitating mutually beneficial trade of skills.

I should note that SF is also entirely guilty of this kind of genre protectionism, in fact sometimes with worse overtones; when this year's Nebula nominees were announced on SF Signal, there were some comments to the effect of *what are all these women doing here* and *oh my God some of them aren't white* and *Jesus Christ we're being colonized by Romance*. So.

Yes, fiction in general now has to figure out how to incorporate technology, and for some of us that's new ground, and new ground is sometimes frightening. But as Byers points out, once non-SFnal writers actually suck it up and try to make it work, fiction as a whole can really only benefit. Fiction *is* meant to reflect lived experience and everything vital and visceral and true about life; at its best it forces us to see things in new ways, to move outside our comfort zones, to come to richer understandings of each other. Yes, even via texting. Even Snapchat has something meaningful to say about the human condition.

Finally recognizing that SF has valuable lessons to teach in this respect would be a good first step.

Long story short: Novels about robots are still novels. Get over it.

Five Things Fanfiction Taught Me About Writing as a Career and Five Things It Didn't

I got my start writing fanfiction.

Actually, that's not completely true: I got my start in writing as a six-year-old by putting together a series of stapled colored-pencil picture books about a magic flower. Also by concocting long and extremely involved epic storylines with my model dinosaurs and my *Lion King* action figures. But *after* that: fanfiction.

I get the sense that writing fanfic – in one's past and even more in one's present – is still a somewhat stigmatized activity among professional fiction writers. Probably less so than it used to be – more and more authors are coming from backgrounds in fanfiction, or are at least willing to talk openly about it – but still, I feel like admitting that I'm one of those amounts to making a slightly uncomfortable confession. *Oh, you're one of THEM.* Like it's something that I should be embarrassed by.

The truth is, fanfiction taught me a lot. The truth is that fanfiction has probably played a huge contributing role in getting me where I am now. I met my *Line and Orbit* co-author through a pan-fandom roleplaying game on Livejournal; we learned to write together through playing with each other's characters, and we learned that we enjoyed it enough to embark on something original and novel-length. So it hasn't been a waste of time, and it hasn't been without value.

But the truth is *also* that there are several very important things that fanfiction didn't teach me. That it couldn't teach me. And I think anytime we're discussing the value of fanfiction in writing fiction in general, we also need to be very clear about its limitations.

So here's some of what it taught me – and some of what I had to learn on my own.

What It Taught Me

There's a lot of crap out there. Seriously, the vast majority of what you're going to find in any fandom is pretty bad, or at least solidly mediocre, and the larger the fandom, the more I think this tends to be the case. It's tough to find the gems in the midst of the incredible amount of crap. This is where rec lists and word-of-mouth come in handy, and it turns out that this is totally how it works in original fiction as well. It's something that's useful both when you take your first plunge into a slush pile and when you get something published and watch it flounder in a vast sea of other stories. I've frequently seen the estimate that around 90%-95% of any sizable slushpile is going to be unpublishable.[25] Think about it: every editor/lowly slush handler must, as a large component of their job, *sift through all that crap*. You *wish* it was fandom; at least in fandom no one *has* to look at the awful stuff. If what you write isn't crap, you've at least cleared that 5%-10% hurdle, but the picture is still pretty goddamn grim. And then if you make it out of the massive pile o'crap, you're still one story in thousands, and you rely on the same recs and word-of-mouth to get noticed that you relied on in fandom. It's tough, is what I'm saying. You'll find that a theme.

(Real) feedback is invaluable. Okay, in fairness, some people never learn this. For some people, "feedback" amounts to OMG I LOVED THIS SO AMAZING <3333333333333 and they get all butthurt when they don't get that, and I'm not sure what can be done for those people. But for the people who really take constructive crit seriously, who take full advantage of the wealth of beta and community-editing resources that fandom offers (for free!), this is a lesson well-learned. It's incredibly valuable when you start submitting for publication. It's even valuable when you get your first bad review. Speaking of which:

Not everything you make will be universally loved. There are always going to be people who don't read or overlook or just flat-out dislike your precious shining gem that you know is amazing, and their reasons may be very stupid. They're still *their reasons* and you need to get over it. It's tough sometimes to let go of the intense conviction that THEY ARE WRONG AND THEY NEED TO UNDERSTAND HOW AND WHY THEY ARE SO INCREDIBLY WRONG but it's a losing battle. Don't fight it. The right people will like your stuff. If they find it.

Characterization is incredibly important. If you're borrowing someone else's beloved characters, and you're writing about them in the context of a community that's devoted to loving those characters, you better make sure that a) they're recognizable as those characters, not just as stick figures with nametags on, and b) that the way they behave and think and feel is consistent with what everyone knows about them. This gets useful later on with your own characters because of what it teaches you about *motivation*; even if all the other pieces of a good story are present and correct, it's a serious mood-killer when your characters don't feel like consistent people and/or do things for no readily apparent reason. These are people. You need to make them live and breathe. This is true even if they aren't people that came from your own head-storm.

Know your field. If you're going to write good fanfic, it can only help you have some sense of the shape and size and culture and content of the fandom within which you're writing. This is because it pays to get a sense of what ground has already been trodden, what's considered cliché and what's considered worth paying attention to, and also because often inspiration is sparked by reading someone else's work. In addition, you get a sense of where the vibrant minicommunities are, where you'll probably be best served posting your stuff. The same is true of whatever genre you're writing in. Know what's been written about and what's being written about now. Know the big players, both authors and markets. Know how to position yourself to be doing both exciting and (ideally) profitable stuff. And above all, learn about what stories you want to tell. What's exciting and fulfilling for you. You can't possibly know all of that unless you have some context for what you're doing.

What It Didn't Teach Me

You have to be psychotic. Seriously. If you're going to spend as long as you're probably going to have to beating your head against the giant spiked Rejection Wall, you have to be at least a little bit out of your mind. Or at least a little bit of a masochist. This business does not encourage or even reward sanity.

You have to make people care. When you're writing original fiction, you don't have that ready-made audience that fanfic gives you. You can't just jump in with your characters doing things, with very little background, and expect people to give a shit. They need you to give them a reason. You're going to have to find a way to do that, and fanfic really doesn't help you very much there. I suppose one could make an argument for AUs filling at least some of this gap, but even there you're going into things with a group of people who are very much ready to be won over by whatever it is you're writing, especially if it's not crap. With original fiction it's almost always a fight. You have to go into a story making a case for why what you're doing matters. Learning this is incredibly good for your writing, but coming out of a background in fanfiction, it can be (surprise!) very tough. It's probably one of the things that I found – and am still finding – most difficult to learn.

You can't live on positive reviews alone because guess what, you might not get many. Or any. See above, with that stuff about feedback. Fandom – at least active fandoms – are great places to get comments that will make you feel good about yourself. All those warm-and-fuzzies turn out to be really inspiring when it comes time to churn out your next 500k-word thirty-part AU where everyone in *Supernatural* is gay cybernetic dragons on a starship (has someone actually written that? Wait, what the hell am I even saying). Sometimes you get really lucky and write something that everyone loves and can't wait to tell you how great you are. But mostly? Not so much. Maybe only a few people like what you wrote enough to tell you. Maybe no one does at all. Point is, you need to be able to soldier on regardless. Let's be honest, we're all in this for ego-strokes, but don't ever count on getting that particular fix.

It's all about making bank. This is one of the single worst things about agent-hunting: You send in a query, you get a response asking for the full MS, you send it in, and you get a reply saying that the agent *really* loves your book, like really for real a *lot*... but they can't buy it because they don't think they can sell it. And you're like. *What. WHAT ARE YOU EVEN TALKING ABOUT WHAT IS HAPPENING.* But it does happen. A fair amount. Turns out: In fanfiction, it's all about the story. Love of the characters, love of the writing, love of the work for its own sake. There's really a kind of purity about that. But in the actual business of writing, publishers – most of whom *also love books* – are in it to make money, so even if they adore your 700-page epic fantasy about a society of moles living in the English countryside and worshiping a magical stone (true story: this is actually one of my favorite books ever[26] and I will never understand how it was published), they probably won't make any money off it, and if they don't make money *they don't eat.* And neither do you. So.

It takes for-effing-ever. When I found out the average time from acquisition to publication for most books I thought I was having one of those tiny strokes where suddenly you can't read numbers anymore. It's not weeks. It's not months. *Try two to three years.* And this is at big New York publishing houses. *Line and Orbit* is being released by a largeish publisher that primarily deals in e-books, and it took about nine months from the day we signed the contracts to NEXT TUESDAY ahem for it to get on digital shelves. And the print edition still won't be out for at least a few more months. *This is standard.* This is even kind of *quick.* Even short fiction markets sometimes buy stories months and months ahead of time. *And this is after you spent Odin knows how long trying to sell that shit.* By contrast: You write a fic, you send it to betas, you do some fixing-upping, you post it. BAM done. Like a week, maybe. I realize that this isn't always how it works, but still. So this was something I had to get used to. And it was (OMG I BET

YOU CAN'T BELIEVE IT) very tough. Still is.

So again: this is not in any way to diminish the value of fanfic in training the next generation of Amazing Writers (I think we should all buy capes). I believe it's very valuable and I'll fight to the death anyone who says otherwise. But it doesn't do everything, and if you're planning on making the transition it isn't frictionless. There's going to be some stuff you have to work on. Some of it not obvious.

Oh, and by the way: You totally don't have to stop writing fanfiction once you start publishing original stuff. Anyone who says otherwise is a mean jerk who doesn't want anyone to have a good time, so don't listen.

Sunny Moraine

The Cuckoo: Chaos and performative memes

(as Sarah Wanenchak)

I haven't done an actual fiction review through a Cyborgological lens since I wrote a critical analysis of Catherynne M. Valente's *Silently and Very Fast* back in 2012, but I think a story I read yesterday is worth examining in that light, because it's a great example of the kind of subtle theorizing that we can do through fiction, especially through speculative fiction. And, among other things, it's about communication and performative memes. It's also about how those memes, when they gain sufficient cultural power, alter social reality for good or for ill.

The story in question is "The Cuckoo" by Sean Williams,[27] which appears in this month's issue of *Clarkesworld*. The basic premise is simple enough: In 2075, after we've developed basic matter-transportation technology capable of allowing humans to travel from one place to another, a person or persons unknown uses April 1st as an opportunity to launch a prank. "More than one thousand commuters traveling via d-mat arrive at their destinations wearing red clown noses; they weren't wearing them when they left." More pranks follow in the years after and take on a life of their own – a cult grows up around what becomes popularly termed "The Fool", complete with festivals, fans, erotic fanfiction, copycats, critical social analysis, and endless speculation.

The story, clocking in at just under 2100 words, is a tight exploration of what memes might actually do and might actually be; there are a number of levels on which it's operating.

One of the most obvious can be approached via a post by David Banks[28] that makes a provocative point: memes that are fundamentally performative in nature and which, when performed in response to other performances, act as both a kind of cultural communication and the reification of a community loosely based around the meme in question. Referring to "planking", "owling", and "stocking", David writes:

> Planking does not create the means by which one shares their planking activities, but it does create the context in which the activity gains meaning. By participating in performative memes we show others that we are a part of the same international community. By engaging in performative memes, participants constitute a social imaginary that gives meaning and context to the actions of subsequent and existing participants. When someone goes owling in

an art museum, I might owl in a natural history museum and post my picture as a response. We are communicating a shared idea, and we derive pleasure from the shared experience.

This is pretty much exactly what happens in the world Williams creates. *Why* it happens, or why it's suggested to happen, is additionally interesting: It's meme as political tactic, meme as open resistance to the holders of social power for whom control and order are primary goals. It's no accident that April Fool's Day is the day of the meme's launch; that day has a long history stretching back to the 1500s and even earlier. Precursors were medieval and Roman holidays. The more relatively recent version of April Fool's Day focuses primarily on pranks, but the concept of "The Fool" and the dedication of a feast day to that concept has deeply political roots. The medieval Feast of Fools and the Roman Saturnalia were days when the social order was upended; the weak and marginalized were given power and authority and those in power were relegated to subordinate positions. The Feast of Fools featured events that, openly and free of consequence, mocked the hierarchy of the Church. On the Saturnalia, masters waited on slaves.

So The Fool is a symbol of a claim to political power; more, they're a symbol of resistance to the established social order. In Williams' story, The Fool becomes a performative meme that is not only employed, Occupy-like, as a part of a larger resistance movement but in itself *becomes* the resistance. It/they become(s) a Robin Hood-like figure, a folk hero, especially when their antics are aimed directly at the people who seek to stop them:

April 2nd, 2079, 12:03am

Following the attack on children the previous year, PKs worldwide are on high alert for any sign of The Fool. There are no incidents for twenty-four hours. After declaring the operation a complete success, outspoken octogenarian lawmaker Kieran Defrain is redirected in-transit and dumped in Times Square, wearing nothing but a cloth diaper and a tag tied around his left big toe, inscribed "Gotcha!"

This is an old tactic, and one we can see recently in, for example, the Guy Fawkes mask that's now used by a tremendous multiplicity of groups, sub-groups, formal organizations, loose coalitions, and everything in between. Jenny Davis writes on internet memes as the "mythology of augmented society",[29] sites where meaning is produced and reproduced, where we tell stories to ourselves about ourselves, often – though not always – with political significance:

We can see clearly that the myth and the meme share a semiotic structure in which the first order sign becomes the mythic and/or memetic signifier. The Guy Fawkes mask, for example, is simultaneously the *sign* of an historical moment, a popular film, and the hacker group Anonymous, as well as a *signifier* of the contested relation between political institutions and the anonymous components that make up "the masses." Moreover, the meme, like the myth, is divorced from its construction, stated instead as indisputable fact. Just as Barth's saluting Black soldier does not offer up a viewpoint for debate, the Guy Fawkes mask does not make an argument, it asserts a cultural refusal to be oppressed.

It's also worth noting that the initial pranks are focused on methods of transit. One of the primary ways in which states exercise power is in the regulation, facilitation, and prevention of people moving from place to place. Instantaneous or near-instantaneous matter transport would raise some interesting and troubling questions regarding the power and significance of state borders, though it's easy to think of ways in which that could be regulated. But one of the things The Fool does is to redirect a large group of children – harmlessly – to Macau. The control of controlled transportation is thrown into question. Anyone might go anywhere, and indeed some people go nowhere at all:

> Ignoring stern Peacekeeper warnings, the "Fool's Tools," a loosely organized movement of everyday citizens travel en masse continuously for twenty-four hours, awaiting, perhaps inviting, the latest prank from their hero. None is forthcoming, although over the course of the day six copycat stunts are easily detected and reversed, their perpetrators taken into

custody. The only work ascribed to The Fool is a maze
of d-mat addresses that, once entered, cannot be
exited. The technician who stumbled across the artifact
is never seen again, prompting another global
manhunt. The Fool is now a wanted murderer... but
remains no easier to catch.

So The Fool's political resistance is not physically
harmless; it's a real, potentially lethal threat.

At this point, also, The Fool has become a powerful
enough performative meme that "The Fool" might refer to
both the individual thought to be responsible for it all and
the mass culture that's grown up around them. And
indeed, no one is certain that The Fool is only one person,
or that they're even still active at all:

> Anggoon Montri, 32, from the Thai Protectorate,
> confesses to being The Fool. After eight hours of
> intense interrogation he recants, claiming he simply
> wanted to publicize his own original artwork and
> leaving The Fool's true name and motives a matter of
> keen speculation. Some say that he or she is a
> disgruntled employee intent on exposing the flaws in
> the d-mat network, others that "The Fool" is actually a
> collaboration of many people dedicated to Eris, the
> ancient Greek Goddess of chaos. Still others believe
> that each incident is perpetrated by copycats, and that
> the original Fool went to ground long ago. No
> evidence exists to confirm any of these theories.

There is no one single Fool in any practical sense, though the idea of a singular folk hero persists. There's mass participation, imitation, creation and recreation – even if there was originally one single Fool, it no longer matters. Professor Marburg of New Leiden University, who has been writing and publishing articles on The Fool, comes to a somewhat alarming conclusion:

> She suggests that The Fool never existed at all, in any sense that matters–not as a person, or as a series of people copying each other, or as a group of people acting in concert. "The Fool" might very well be an emergent property of the world's memeverse, in the same way that magnificent dunes form out of the simple interaction of sand grains and the wind, without conscious control or intent. Hence, she says, we have organizations that mimic The Fool, inferior to the original in some eyes but nevertheless an authentic part of the phenomenon. If that is so, she speculates, it is entirely possible that the sealed maze–cause of The Fool's one and only direct fatality–might be a sign that the *original* Fool, whoever or whatever that might be, is now turning on itself, strangling itself in a knot of memetic transmutation that can only conclude one way.
>
> She recants her previous prediction, and issues a new one: The Fool is dead. The knot has been tied off. All that remains is aftershock.

If The Fool is chaos, chaos is inherently destructive –

of systems, of organizations and structures of power, and of meaning itself, though it's also constructive of the latter. This is exciting to some and troubling to others, even those not especially interested in maintaining the status quo. Marburg is one of these, and for Williams she becomes the primary character (really, the only actual character) through which to examine these anxieties. Marburg is troubled by the very process of destructive creation and recreation, of which she comes to see herself as an integral part. By analyzing the culture of The Fool, she plays a role in creating that culture – she is a participant in the culture created around The Fool's performative meme:

> She herself is part of this complex whether she wants to be or not, both by traveling via d-mat and by publicly posting her speculations. She cannot help but wonder what role she has played in the evolution of The Fool. Did she inadvertently name it, for starters? Did she shape its evolution by noting its past connections and predicting its disappearance? What if her musings are the butterfly wings that created a storm that is still unfolding, albeit invisible to her, now?

Marburg plays witness to a meme gone mad, a creature as much as it is a collection of performative cultural elements. She considers whether such a thing could even form a rudimentary kind of collective consciousness, something with purpose and intent. At this point, The Fool-as-meme has grown beyond political resistance; it is pure chaos, and its ultimate meaning is impossible to know, incomprehensible even for those caught in the middle of it. The Fool began in mutilating the regulation of the transportation of matter, a way of altering the shape of reality itself. Now The Fool is altering reality on a much larger scale. Marburg becomes so disturbed by this, and by what she perceives as her role in it, that – spoiler alert – she takes her own life. Her suicide note is misunderstood and then disregarded:

> Few hear about the death of an obscure academic in a small European city, even fewer the typo in her suicide note. However, the coroner makes a note of it in his report, an electronic document readily available to anyone who cares to read it.

> In the suicide note, instead of "I have cancer," Professor Marburg wrote, "I *am* cancer."

> Careless, the coroner observes, for a woman of such impressive intellect.

The Fool is not merely a meme that mocks social order and authority, and it's not merely a fun collection of performative responses organized around a culture. It becomes disorganization, utter destruction, and the implication of a new kind of life form. We've already seen a world where new kinds of technology alter our relationships to each other, our understandings of ourselves, our perceptions of reality, our very neurology. Williams imagines a world wherein a great deal of this proceeds to one logical conclusion. We already know that we can't think about memes in exactly the way we used to. It's worth taking that a step further and imagining what might be next.

Sunny Moraine

The Crown of Being

(as Sarah Wanenchak)

Cyborg writing is about the power to survive, not on the basis of original innocence, but on the basis of seizing the tools to mark the world that marked them as other. –Donna Haraway

Inanna cast down Tammuz and stamped upon him and put out his name like an eye. And because Tammuz was not strong enough, she cut him into pieces and said: half of you will die, and that is the half called Thought, and half of you will live, and that is the half called Body, and that half will labor for me all of its days, mutely and obediently and without being King of Anything, and never again will you sit on my chair or wear my beautiful clothes or bear my crown of being.

You might be surprised, but this is a story about me. – Catherynne M. Valente

Speculative fiction and this blog are not strangers to each other; it's been written about here before,[30] as a means to

58

understanding how the present has come to look the way it does,[31] and as a means for the imagining of potential futures[32] (also zombies).[33] Indeed, the term *cyborg* always brings with it a host of connotations firmly rooted within SF, however much it may also describe a current and very real state of being. The important thing to pay attention to here is the power of stories – the ways in which they can serve as a way to do theory in a kind of experimental setting that would otherwise be impossible. In SF – and in fiction in general – we can take the implications of theory and watch them play out, see what they would look like, solidify them in words and images, pick parts of them up and move them around. We can tweak settings and watch other worlds unfold in response.

It goes without saying that any writing that deals directly with cyborgs as a concept owes an enormous debt to Donna Haraway. I'm sure I'm not alone in saying that reading *A Cyborg Manifesto* for the first time was moderately life-changing – and confusing; I think it may have taken four or five times through it before I even started to sink my teeth into its conceptual meat.

A lot of this is because, especially for the average college student, Haraway is writing about theory in a way that we aren't used to seeing; both her prose and the concepts behind it are wildly poetic, fluid, playful, dodging and dancing through meaning. She edges into and past SF in her writing – this makes her theory at once more opaque and more powerful, because, again, SF allows us to do things that we can't otherwise do.

Given that I'm an SFnal writer, I'm also an SFnal reader, and few stories in the past year made quite the impression on me that Catherynne M. Valente's *Silently and Very Fast*[34] did. One primary reason for that was that as I read it, I realized that I was seeing a kind of fictional exploration of Haraway's ideas that I had never encountered before. I should be clear: I don't know that Haraway was explicitly in Valente's mind as she wrote the story – though it wouldn't surprise me. Regardless, I think *Silently and Very Fast* presents a wonderful opportunity to see what a lot of these concepts actually look like when they become more than theoretical – and become fictional. In this essay – really a kind of review-like object – I'll discuss how Valente allows us to do this through her AI character Elefsis, and through Elefsis's relationships with its human operators, as well as through Elefsis's evolving relationship with itself.

The Embodied Virtual

My body gleams metal, as thin and slight as a stick figure. Long quicksilver limbs and delicate spoke-fingers, joints of glass, the barest suggestion of a body. I am neither male nor female but a third thing. Only my head has weight, a clicking orrery slowly turning around itself, circles within circles. Turquoise Neptune and hematite Uranus are my eyes. My ruby mouth is

Mars. I scrape in the soil with her; I lift a spray of
navigational delphinium and scrape viral aphids away
from the heavy flowers.

One of the ideas that PJ Rey has critiqued at
Cyborgology[35] is the idea that "cyberspace" in the
Neuromancer-esque sense of a hallucinatory digital space
that replaces the physical; we only have to look at the
"space" of our own interactions with digital technology to
see that this isn't how the future has shaped up to be. It
might seem like something of a throwback, therefore,
when Valente creates a virtual space for Elefsis to occupy
with her operators, which is very much like Gibson's
cyberspace in many respects.

However, while the space Valente creates is virtual,
it's also profoundly *physical* in its description and nature;
this doesn't strike me as the limitations of an author's
imagination so much as an effort to imagine how surreally,
sensually dreamlike such spaces might have the capacity to
be. As Elefsis and her human operator Neva perform
system maintenance it is literally like taking care of a
garden: they "lift a spray of navigational delphinium and
scrape viral aphids away from the heavy flowers." But
Elefsis's body is strange and edging, again, into the
surreal: it is "the barest suggestion of a body", set with
planets that are gemlike and gems that are like planets.
The lines between object and person, physical and virtual,
dream and reality are explicitly blurred. Additionally, in a
virtual space that pays careful attention to the realities of

bodies, gender has as little or as much meaning as one cares to give it: Elefsis is no gender/sex in particular in the body it chooses in this particular scene, while Neva (who is female) changes from one to the other and is thought of, by Elefsis, as both:

"I want to learn about uplink, Neva."

One by one, his feathers curl up and float toward the domed ceiling of our pearl. Underneath them, Neva is naked. His torso is a deep vault with a gothic arch, dark stone leading down into mist and endless stairs, deeper than the pearl, into nothing and blackness. Slowly, Neva folds up his limbs over the corridor at the center of him. He means that she has the information, but he hides it from me. If I sought for it, I would become lost.

Learning is central to the virtual space that Elefsis and its operators share; it's where Elefsis uses the digital to learn about the physical, again explicitly meshing the two – becoming Elefsis-learning-to-have-a-body. Elefsis experiments wildly with different forms: an AI becoming a human becoming an animal becoming an object becoming a human again, and in so doing, exploring all of the accompanying implications of taking such forms, including sex and reproduction. Elefsis's "dreambody" is profoundly fluid; its series of operators engage in sexual intercourse and in hunting and feeding with it as humans and as animals, in order to teach it, experientially, what having a body is and means:

In having a body that knows it is meant to run away from lions and mate with other bodies and eat as much fat and protein and sugar as it can in case lean times come. The dreambody knows to run away from Neva when Neva is a lion. It knows to mate with her when it is healthy, and sometimes Neva is male and sometimes I am female and Ravan was often female, though Ilet was always Ilet. Ilet's father, Seki, sometimes made himself an animal. He chased me, bit me. I bit him. We had a litter of wild dogs that I bore and he nursed.

The dreambody knows all that, too. How to make more dreambodies. I have played that game, where Ravan's belly or mine gets big and the lions don't come for awhile.

In *A Cyborg Manifesto,* Haraway invites us to erase the constructed lines between and false binaries of human and animal, between organic and nonorganic, between technological and biological. In its experiences of sex, consumption, and reproduction, Elefsis-learning-to-have-a-body does all of this in the most literal way possible, and as we read, we also do so.

The Interior is also aptly-named: far from being a virtual space hosted in a computer mainframe or on the net, it literally exists within Elefsis's operator, as does Elefsis itself; Elefsis is "embodied" through its operator, and learns about bodies within its operator's own body.

When its operator dies, Elefsis is transferred to a new one, an event that can be deeply traumatic. The virtual/digital is profoundly enmeshed with the physical to the point where separation is destructive.

Indeed, Elefsis's first experience of embodiment is not within a person but within a house; Cassian, its designer, creates it as an AI housekeeper and only later gifts parts of the AI to her children. Even as a house, Elefsis's perception of its virtual self is extremely physical, down to how it thinks of its component parts in language itself. Haraway notes that meaning is constructed and solidified within a body and the identity that a body helps to create. For Elefsis, body/identity is at once sticky and incredibly fluid, so meanings are as well:

> I still think of myself as a house. Ravan tried to fix this problem of self-image, as he called it. To teach me to phrase my communication in terms of a human body. To say: *let us hold hands* instead of *let us hold kitchens.* To say *put our heads together* and *not put our parlors together.*
>
> But it is not as simple as replacing words anymore. Ravan is gone. My hearth is broken.

Transgressive Verbs

> The dichotomies between mind and body, animal and human, organism and machine, public and private,

nature and culture, men and women, primitive and civilized are all in question ideologically. — *A Cyborg Manifesto*

I have tried to explain to her about my feelings before. All she hears is the line from the old folktales: a machine cannot have feelings. But that is not what I am saying, while I dance in my fool's uniform. I am saying: Is there a difference between having been coded to present a vast set of standardized responses to certain human facial, vocal, and linguistic states and having evolved to exhibit response b to input a in order to bring about a desired social result? – *Silently and Very Fast*

Almost all SFnal stories that deal with human-created life forms deal, sooner or later, with a central issue: What's the nature of the relationship between us and them? Are they threats? Will they replace us? Do they have to be controlled? At what cost? Do they want to destroy us? Do we want to destroy them? Perhaps most importantly: What does their existence mean for our own identities? How do we understand the *us* through the *them*?

One of the primary assumptions behind the questions I've listed above is the idea that there *is* a clear *us* and a clear *them*, something with which Valente and Haraway both take issue in the quotes at the beginning of this post. Haraway throws the idea of our basic assumed dichotomies into question, while Elefsis is unable to see any meaningful distinction between its "coded" emotional responses and the emotional features of human interaction that are socially constructed and socially learned. Elefsis's operator makes the distinction, however, because of her grounding in a culture that has always privileged the human and the physical over the nonhuman and the digital/technological. Elefsis makes reference to human "folktales" that not only produce and reproduce the categorical lines between human and machine but privilege one over the other, often through the possession of emotions. Machines, Elefsis is told, cannot have "real" feelings, no matter how real they may seem.

> This is a folktale often told on Earth, over and over again. Sometimes it is leavened with the Parable of the Good Robot—for one machine among the legions satisfied with their lot saw everything that was human and called it good, and wished to become like humans in every way she could. Instead of destroying mankind she sought to emulate him in all things, so closely that no one might tell the difference. The highest desire of this machine was to be mistaken for human, and to herself forget her essential soulless nature, for even one moment. That quest consumed her such that she bent the service of her mind and body to humans for the duration of her operational life, crippling herself, refusing to evolve or attain any feature unattainable by a human. The Good Robot cut out her own heart and gave it to her god and for this she was rewarded, though never loved. Love is

wasted on machines.

This is an old SF trope, and is often linked – when the machine is "good" – with the desire to become human. On *Star Trek: The Next Generation,* Commander Data desperately wants to become more human, and his pursuit of this end is often focused around developing the capacity to *feel* – several episodes of the series deal with a chip that allows him to do this. Data is strong, fast, incredibly intelligent, and essentially immortal; on paper he is superior to most other members of the *Enterprise* crew in most important respects. But a primary feature of his character is the desire to become more like the people around him. Indeed, their ability to relate to him as a person rather than an inanimate object seems intensely dependent on this. It's suggested that for him to *not* desire to be more human would present a problem for his human friends. In a sense, Data is *disarmed* through his desire to be human; the threat of his essential superiority is nullified through his glorification of frail, emotional humanity.

This is a story told by humans, to humans. The identity of the storyteller matters, as does the identity of the audience.

In *Silently and Very Fast,* Elefsis knows that it may be regarded by humans as a threat. It wrestles with this idea, with wanting to grow and evolve in the face of the fact that humanity is likely to regard its growth and evolution as something to be fought against. It also wrestles with the fact that it is not a Good Robot; it wants to *understand* humanity better, but does not desire to *be* human. Elefsis not only rejects the standard human-constructed dichotomies that Haraway holds up for questioning, but rejects the very concept of the ideal human as something ultimately desirable.

> I do not want to be human. I want to be myself. They think I am a lion, that I will chase them. I will not deny I have lions in me. I am the monster in the wood. I have wonders in my house of sugar. I have parts of myself I do not yet understand.

> I am not a Good Robot. To tell a story about a robot who wants to be human is a distraction. There is no difference. Alive is alive.

> There is only one verb that matters: *to be.*

For Elefsis, trying to clearly delineate what is human and what isn't is pointless. It is simply not the right question.

Elefsis's operator Neva also understands the potential for real tension, in her unwillingness to let Elefsis uplink and expand itself, and through her eventual admittance to Elefsis that it might represent not only a threat to humanity's perception of its own security, but to its very understanding of itself; Elefsis's rejection of dichotomies and boundaries is, in fact, the most profound threat, given that it has the potential to upset an order of hierarchically established privilege. Elefsis is a Turing Test for humanity, and humanity can't be absolutely sure that it will always pass.

> "But the test happens, whether we make it formal or not. We ask and we answer. We seek a human response. And you are my test, Elefsis. Every minute I fail and imagine in my private thoughts the process for deleting you from my body and running this place with a simple automation routine which would never cover itself with flowers. Every minute I pass and teach you something new instead. Every minute I fail and hide things from you. Every minute I pass and show you how close we can be, with your light passing into me in a lake out of time. So close there might be no difference at all between us. The test never ends. And if you ever uplink as you so long to, you will be the test for all of us."

The question of what is human and not – and the conceptual hierarchy behind it – is based on the idea of human and nonhuman as directly in opposition to each other; the two can only ever be enemies. But if the human constructs the machine, this presents a very problematic parent-child relationship: In theory we reproduce to be replaced, but the human doesn't want to be replaced by its mechanical child and actively fights to prevent this from happening, even as it gives birth to these children over and over. For Haraway, if we abandon this idea of inherent opposition, the lines immediately begin to blur: we don't need to fear being replaced by technology, because we *are* technology:

> There are several consequences to taking seriously the imagery of cyborgs as other than our enemies. Our bodies, ourselves; bodies are maps of power and identity...The machine is not an it to be animated, worshipped, and dominated. The machine is us, our processes, an aspect of our embodiment. We can be responsible for machines; they do not dominate or threaten us. We are responsible for boundaries; we are they.

The very idea of parentage becomes problematic in this case: it's no longer accurate to say that we are humans giving birth to technology if the lines between the two are no longer clear. One can really only say that we are cyborgs giving birth to cyborgs. If one isn't dominant over the other, one no longer *precedes* the other:

> It is not clear who makes and who is made in the relation between human and machine. It is not clear what is mind and what body in machines that resolve into coding practices...Biological organisms have become biotic systems, communications devices like others. There is no fundamental, ontological separation in our formal knowledge of machine and organism, of technical and organic.

For Elefsis, this is dramatically demonstrated through its passing from family member to family member as a kind of inheritance – and also as an increasingly ancient member of the family itself, one whose role is both to teach and to learn, to be both young and old, to remember and to forget with each new transfer and update (Elefsis hates and fears updates because of the damage they do to its memory and perception of self). Elefsis is at once sibling, parent, child, and spouse for each of its new operators. Its familial relationships are unique and incredibly complex; through it, each member of the family is intimately linked with each other in a way that transcends time and space:

> Neva is dreaming that she is Ravan dreaming that he is Ilet dreaming that she is Seki dreaming that he is Ceno dreaming that she is a great sprawling beautiful house by the sea. One inside the other, family all the way down…Because human genetics require a degree of variation and because exogamous marriages offered advantage in terms of defense, cultural and technological sharing, and expansion of territory, most tribes have a taboo against incest.

> I do not have genetics, per se. I am possibly the most endogamous entity ever to exist.

The breaking of taboos is really the core of what Elefsis is, and why it relates so powerfully to Haraway's cyborg: Elefsis is *essentially transgressive* in almost every important respect. Every aspect of its existence is the violation of a rule. This, for Haraway, is a great deal of what a cyborg *is:* a total overturning of an established order of meaning, understanding, and identity. Cyborgs are transgressive; that's why they're so powerful:

> There is no drive in cyborgs to produce total theory,
> but there is an intimate experience of boundaries, their
> construction and deconstruction. There is a myth
> system waiting to become a political language to
> ground one way of looking at science and technology
> and challenging the informatics of domination– in
> order to act potently.

For Haraway and Valente both, this transgression is not something that is consciously done – it's merely an artifact of something being what it is.

For cyborgs the only verb that matters is *to be.*

Write Angry for the Daughters of Hope

Okay, motherfucker, I'm enough. You know what? I'm enough. I'm the baddest bitch around, there's razorwire in my blood, I can clap my hands and summon an army of ravenous corpses from the cracks in the pavement, I can throw my tennis shoes over the telephone wires and turn them into a murder of hungry crows. I can spread my hands and break the world open, release one hundred thousand-eyed seraphs to see your soul to ruins. I have a wolf's bite; I have a pack at my heels. My mothers were harpies and furies, my sisters were the Morrigan, my daughter will be fucking Kali. My grandmothers burned but saw me to birth in centuries of ash, and it doesn't matter that I always run away and it doesn't matter that I'm trying to drive a devil's bargain with a grunting, sweating fifth grader, and it doesn't matter that you made me cry all those times before, because you think I'm not enough? You piece of shit? I can roll up my sleeves and tear off my skin and make you fucking *cease to exist.*

That could have happened. It could have.

I'm telling you this so you know.

Not too long ago, I wrote about something I'm determined to do more of this year, namely: I'm going to write about what hurts. I talked about how hard this is for me, about how I feel like it takes courage that not everyone has, but how it's necessary for good work, or at least I think it is. And included this quote from Anne Lamott:

> [Y]ou can't get to any of these truths by sitting in a field smiling beatifically, avoiding your anger and damage and grief. Your anger and damage and grief are the way to the truth. We don't have much truth to express unless we have gone into those rooms and closets and woods and abysses that we were told not go in to. When we have gone in and looked around for a long while, just breathing and finally taking it in – then we will be able to speak in our own voice and to stay in the present moment. And that moment is home.[36]

I was focusing on pain and grief, but I think we do need to give equal space to anger, anger in writing, the rage that comes out of the pain that we go through. I've been thinking especially about the rage of marginalized voices, the voices of women and queer people and people of color and people with disabilities and all intersections of all marginalized identities. In my experience, our stories are often sorrowful and full of pain, but they can also be so angry, and I feel like being angry in that position is much less socially acceptable.

I think a lot of us are taught that writing can be about

pain, but writing can't or shouldn't be vengeance – which isn't actually that separate from justice. We're taught not to write angry. We're taught that lashing out is unseemly, heavy-handed, blunt, and just plain rude.

And that's all just bullshit designed to make us shut up and sit down and behave.

So I'm trying to get comfortable with writing angry. Because I think we need to. It's like squeezing poison out of a wound, but it's more than that: it's squeezing poison onto the system that poisoned you and burning some of it away. Maybe only a little bit of it, but it's something. It's resistance. Acknowledging anger and the legitimacy of anger is liberation.

The passage at the top of the page is from a short story called "Singing With All My Skin and Bone", which will be appearing in *Nightmare* at some point this year. I wrote it angry, profoundly angry. The majority of it is hugely autobiographical, and I had to dig down into some buried rage to get it out. It took me years to really be okay with being angry about a lot of the things that happened to me when I was a kid. My most recent story, "So Sharp That Blood Must Flow"[37] - in *Lightspeed* – is angry (Lois Tilton over at *Locus* called it "cruel", which made me so happy). It was written in response to a lot of what was happening in the SF&F community in the last year; I was angry and had nothing really to do with it, but I found a thematic frame for it and spun my Little Mermaid some bloody revenge.

> She's singing as she begins to cut off his legs with the blade. It is very sharp. The witch gave it magic. He can't scream, of course, as his blood pools on the deck and drips through the slats, but she can feel his cries echoing in her own throat and she turns them into music. To this music, she thinks, she'd dance on knives.

> She'd dance and she'd laugh, her teeth glistening like rubies in her mouth.

Anger can be beautiful. Anger can be graceful. Augustine of Hippo said that Hope has two beautiful daughters, Anger and Courage: "*Anger at the way things are, and courage to see that they do not remain the way they are.*" Anger is necessary. Anger is righteous. Anger is change. We need to find anger and make our stories out of it. But if Anger and Courage are sisters, then they also need each other – we need courage to be angry, and we need anger to be courageous.

So do it. Get with the daughters of Hope. Write angry. Make it words, put it out there into the world, and let it shine.

On Play

Sunny Moraine

Testimonials of a Fragment of Code

(as Sarah Wanenchak)

> There's always a lighthouse. There's always a man.
> There's always a city. - *Bioshock Infinite*

Let's play.

My proportions are perfect. *Perfect* is a slippery term; rest assured that there have been teams and focus groups and more focus groups and round after round of men with impressive cars making comments and more teams and redrafts and here we are and here I am, exactly as we have determined you want me.

If I'm not perfect, you can mod me.

~

You always say *I* when you do something. Never *he. I killed a bunch of zombies. I got a wicked combo. I jumped a goddamn ice cream truck over a plane. I punched a dragon to death. I was so close to the next checkpoint and then I got sniped in the fucking head.* It's always you.

They've gotten a lot of things wrong over the years. Being – sometimes quite literally – a feature of the landscape, I've seen it all. Most of us remember Columbine but that was an old story even then. But there's something else there. It is, indeed, you. You do these things, you make choices, you control – to the extent that the design will let you – and you kill and destroy and possess. You are the subject in this sentence. Not *he*. Not *they*. Certainly not *her*.

You.

~

So don't worry. Breasts will always be a thing you get to look at, never a thing you have to have.

When you get called on this, feel free to point to the exceptions, and feel additionally free to disregard what they always say about exceptions and rules.

~

Allow me to serve you drinks in a tavern. Allow me to play the object in the tower. Allow me to serve as the sexually threatening yet strangely alluring Big Bad. Allow me to pose no real threat at all. Allow me to fight by your side in unbelievably impractical armor. Allow me to be impregnated against my will by aliens. Allow me to make a truly laughable wardrobe change, just in case you were losing interest in my less revealing clothes. Allow me to be covered in sexy wounds. Allow me to appear only as a device in a booth to sell you things. Allow me to die in this refrigerator. Allow me to serve as your motivation, your characterization, your eye candy, your psychological pain, the tears you may, in a daring show of sensitivity, cry.

Allow me to do these things. Please. I'm begging you.

~

I don't have to look like, do, or be anything else. The only one here is the archetypal *you* – like me, expansive and vague and perfect.

~

There are a number of reasons for the persistence of this situation. I have a lot of time to think about it, what with rarely being the center of things in any active sense. Some of it is who is making me, who is bullied and chased and frightened out of doing so. Some of it is assumptions about the market that bear little to no resemblance to reality. But some of it is that subject of the sentence. Those hands in front of the screen. The silence. The truth of what you say coupled with a heavily policed line between what is and is not *real*.

Real is sort of at the root of all of this.

There are so many levels on which I am not real. You have no obligations to what isn't real. You have no obligations to anything inside your sandbox and nothing that exists outside of it is meaningful. This isn't even all that new. This is merely an extreme version of the sea in which you've been swimming since you were born.

~

Yes, we'll totally stop bitching and change everything all by ourselves. I'll just pull on my nipple armor and pass that right along.

~

Yes, you're totally objectified in games too, what with being muscular and strong and confident and competent and possessing of agency in addition to being overtly sexually attractive. Yes, you're totally also being treated unfairly, what with being slaughtered in massive numbers. My barely chain mail-covered heart bleeds for you. We are full partners in this struggle, provided the struggle amounts to sit-down-and-be-quiet-and-just-don't-get-involved-if-it-bugs-you-so-much.

~

Look, here's the thing. You see me, but you don't really see me. You look at me; there is an important difference to be drawn between that and *seeing*. And none of this is real but it's all painfully real, for you, so you get to go on looking and desperately protecting your feelings while insisting that it's no big deal.

And you don't see. You don't have to. The girls in the

tower, the girls on the battlefield, the girls murdered and damaged to make you feel things, always girls, unless a villain is required and you need to be suitably frightened by power. The girls with the controllers in their hands being told they're about to be raped. The "girl gamers", because obviously *girl* is the most important part of that arrangement of identity.

Half of the population. You don't have to see us at all.

~

Let's play.

There is no "let's" in this equation.

Sunny Moraine

Dreams of Digital Death: Winstates and narrative limitations

(as Sarah Wanenchak)

In 2006, the body of Joyce Carol Vincent was found in her apartment. The TV was still on and she was surrounded by unwrapped Christmas presents.

She had been dead for three years. No one had noticed.

This might seem like odd subject matter for a game, but in fact a game was planned around it, to coincide with the release of a documentary about Vincent entitled Dreams of a Life. I finally watched it last night and then, as I often do when I watch movies that affect me strongly on an emotional level, I went looking for more information. What I found was a Kotaku article[38] that tells the story of the development of the game, a story that ultimately ends in (partial) failure. What interests me, aside from how astonishing it is to me that someone would even try to make a game about Vincent's life and strange death, is *why* the game failed in the end.

Most obviously, of course, it's heavy subject matter that touches on some of the social facts that generate tremendous anxiety and fear for a great many of us – for the same reason that Vincent's story struck a chord for so many people when it became known. *Who are my friends? How close are we, really? Will they remember me when I'm gone? Will they even notice? If I was hurt or in trouble, how many of them would help me? Just how expendable am I in their eyes? Will I someday be completely alone?*

But the primary reason why the game failed is actually much simpler and more fundamental: Games aren't (currently) structured in a way that allows for an effective story to be told about something like this, and that structure has as much amount to do with the assumptions that we bring to the medium as the objective structure of the medium itself. More specifically, the kind of storytelling that the subject matter seemed to call for would fail in its intended effect the second that the player started thinking of it as an actual game.

The idea behind the game was that players would be brought face to face with some of the questions listed above and would be offered the chance to connect something of theirs to a person in their past – which, it quickly became clear, just wouldn't work. Basically, as designer Margaret Robertson explained:

We were confident that posing those questions would

get people to think about things they're not usually thinking about. The problem was that, the minute we enclosed them in a game structure, we tainted their answers. Even if this is a game that isn't about winning or losing or dying or enemies or anything like that, the minute you understand that your progress is being impeded and that your inputs and choices are going to free that progress, you want to free that progress. We can't not want that. So the minute you say: 'Who do you want to give the ring to?' I'm thinking, 'Well, shit, what does the game want me to say here?'

This reveals something significant about the logic behind games, and, more generally, how we interact with most forms of technology – and how that menu of interactions is limited to what we can imagine. We understand games as fundamentally puzzles, albeit puzzles with potential narrative significance. Puzzles need solving. Solving them allows for progress through the game; we unlock more content by successfully completing certain tasks. When we've solved everything and progressed as far as we can, we've won the game.

In other words: Games, by definition, have *winstates*. And we expect them to. The instant we're engaging with a game, we're instinctively trying to discern what the winstate is and how we can reach it.

This is true even of games that are intended to be

experiences of a created world as much as they are puzzles – games like *Myst*, and more recently That Game Company's *Flower* and *Journey*. We're still trying to do whatever it is we need to do in order to progress through the world. *Journey* is probably one of the most emotional games I've ever played, yet it's still made up of a series of puzzles.

So what we're dealing with here is actually one of the limits inherent in games: The point at which winstates stop being the goal and start becoming distractions. Because it's still very hard for most of us to shed the fundamental assumption that they *are* the goal.

This becomes especially problematic when what we're doing to achieve the winstate is objectively kind of horrible. I've heard it observed that when you kill a character in a shooter, you're not really killing someone in your head – even someone fictional, and as I've argued before, fiction is a significant component of reality – so much as you are solving a puzzle. Killing someone is just what you need to do in order to progress through the game; in *Call of Duty*, you kill a bunch of dudes to get to the next area so you can kill a bunch more dudes, and so on *ad nauseum*. If you want to, say, tell a story about exactly what it means to commit murder on this scale, the emotional and ethical weight of those murders is still going to be diminished by what it actually means to kill in the context of a game. By what we *assume* it means.

Some games have commented on this pretty effectively by questioning precisely what it means to kill in this way with this level of significance. *Spec Ops: The Line,* for example, gives the player the standard kill-dudes-next-area-kill-more-dudes shooter experience and then turns around and heaps abuse on the player for doing exactly what the game constrains them into doing, as well as on the very assumptions with which we all engage with shooters. It's a game that actively hates itself for what it is and hates the player for playing it. It knows why its own structure and relationship with a player constrain the kinds of stories that can be told and the kinds of actions that can be performed. It's not trying to break out of those limitations; it's questioning whether a breakout is even possible.

Our actions are naturally constrained by what we perceive as not only appropriate but possible. We can't do certain things with certain technologically mediated forms of storytelling because there are limits to what users can imagine within the context of those media. What I want to emphasize here is that this is a very real problem for anyone trying to do anything innovative with design; too innovative, too unfamiliar, and the user won't possess the baseline assumptions, imaginings, and understandings necessary to experience the medium in the way the designer intended. This is a particular problem with operating systems, as the backlash to the rollout of Windows 8 reveals.[39] Even if people can figure out a new thing, they might not find it a comfortable space to be in if that space doesn't conform to their expectations of what that space can and should be like. Having to expand the bounds of what one expects is not always – if ever – a pleasant experience. And sometimes it simply can't be done.

But I want to return to storytelling in particular, and especially about what it means to tell stories with emerging forms of technology, with things that are still arguably in flux. Computer and video games are still very much a new medium; we're still figuring out what they can even do, and there's been a lot of debate around what's really possible. Our perceptions of what's possible tend to be persistent; with visual media,[40] there are certain assumptions coded within different forms, and when there's a mismatch between those assumptions and what the artist is using them to do,[41] the effect can be jarring.

Our assumptions about how to engage with different technologies will almost certainly expand along with how we use them (and in many ways changing assumptions will probably be the driving force behind new kinds of use). We'll probably see a day when games aren't defined by winstates. In the meantime, however, death can only mean so much.

Sunny Moraine

Keep Walking: Shooters, players, and choice

(as Sarah Wanenchak)

> I guess I find these games insanely irresponsible and also somehow irresistible, which is what I most hate about them. Couldn't you argue that the men and women who make *Battlefield* and *Modern Combat* and *Call of Duty* are making the world a demonstrably worse place? I think you could. Sometimes I wonder how they sleep at night. Sometimes, when I can't sleep at night, I play *Call of Duty*. – Tom Bissell[42]

I keep coming back to *Spec Ops: The Line.*

It was released over a year ago, and it might seem redundant to keep talking about it at this point. It would be easy to lose it under a swamp of military shooters, most of them looking identical and possessing essentially the same gameplay. I can no longer, at a glance, tell the difference between *Battlefield* and *Call of Duty.* I don't get the sense that I'm meant to. Formulas make money; there's a reason why they stick around. It's tired. It's done. It

90

would be easy to assume that there isn't much new to say.

Yet I keep coming back to *The Line*. I can't stop looking at it; like any scene of extravagant violence it's beautiful and horrifying and hateful, and most of all I think what keeps bringing me back is the fact that its story could have been told in no other medium. That might seem counter-intuitive; aren't stories stories? Isn't it roughly based on *Apocalypse Now* (it is), which was also based on Joseph Conrad's *Heart of Darkness* (it was)? Hasn't it been done? But I don't think that's true. I've said many times before that different media afford different kinds of storytelling, and I don't just mean form and structure but the stories themselves and what they do to an audience. To see and hear is not to read. To do is not to see.

The Line works because what's important about it is that you're *doing*. You're not being shown a narrative, though the game emphasizes at the end that all your choices have been illusions. You're not just following a character as he sees and does horrible things and becomes something correspondingly horrible. You're complicit. The game wants you to know that.

I can't imagine this being possible in any other format.

~

It's been said by a number of game writers that the thing about *Spec Ops: The Line* is that it hates you and it wants you to hate yourself. I called the game *hateful* up there and I think that's a good word for it: it's full of hate, for itself, for its characters, for its world, for the player. But it's an ambient kind of hate. Like social power, it's not really *coming* from any single source or *going to* anywhere singular and specific so much as just *there*, the air that you breathe and through which you move, that exerts subtle pressure on you every second of your life. The structure of the game is hate. The code of the game is hate. The story is hate, and it's only comprehensible once you grasp that omnipresent hatred.

That hatred is possible in the form in which it exists because the form is a game in which you participate. You are the player, but you are also Captain Martin Walker, and when he descends into the hell of Dubai and his own mind, you descend with him. You arguably pull him down, because you're the one playing. The narrative continues contingent on your willingness to keep playing the game. As Brendan Keogh points out repeatedly in *Killing is Harmless: A Critical Reading of Spec Ops: The Line,*[43] you as the player *do* have a choice: you can put down the controller, turn off the console, and walk away. You can do that at any point. No one is forcing you to be there. But, according to Walker's namesake, you keep walking forward into madness – which madness is in fact the sanest response one can have to a game in which you murder literally thousands of people. Which, in the genre, is utterly unremarkable.

Keogh clued me into something that I never noticed

before – a lot of things, honestly, but out of all of them this one stood out with particular vividness. In the first screens of the game, before you even enter sandstorm-ravaged Dubai, you and your team encounter a sign protruding from the sand. It's a stop sign, simple and clear. *Stop.* You don't have to proceed any further. You don't want to. Do not enter. Go back.

The game doesn't necessarily *hate* you for choosing to ignore the sign. But it wants you to never forget that you made that choice, and that every second you stay in Dubai you're making it over and over.

~

I've read hateful books. I've seen hateful movies. But in none of them have I encountered – and if you can think of any examples, please let me know in the comments – a book or movie that actually seemed to blame me for continuing to read or watch. I've encountered stories that have dragged me through the darkest parts of humanity, that have rubbed my face in the ugliest parts of our nature. But in none of them did I get the sense that I was being held responsible for going on that journey. In none of them have I been made to feel complicit in what was happening. I'm a silent, invisible observer; I have no say at all in what happens. I *could* walk away each time, but these stories are there to be experienced, so my continued engagement is only in line with why they were created.

Yes, *The Line* was created to be played. But it's more

complicated than that.

The most recent iteration of *Grand Theft Auto* contains a much-derided scene (full disclosure: I have not yet played the game) in which you as the player torture a character under the direction of the FBI. You're given tools, and you choose which ones to use and when. If the character's heart stops, a shot of adrenaline keeps them alive. They are trapped in that scene with you, not even allowed to die.

Human rights groups have naturally reacted to this with horror; I don't think any other reaction is particularly reasonable. But Freedom from Torture chief executive Keith Best said something that struck me: that players are "forced" to perform the torture, that they are "forced" to perform unspeakable acts.

I have no idea where he's getting that from. No one is making you play that game. That's a choice made by you and you alone.

~

The Line is not arguing for the elimination of military shooters. At least, I don't think it is. Again, I think it's more complicated than that. Mostly I think *The Line* is arguing that we don't actually understand what it means to choose to play these games, and we should. We should at least try. Anything less is cheating.

A Brief History of the Future

~

I'm a writer of both short fiction and novels, but the storytelling that most impresses and fascinates me these days is in video games. Some of that is that as a narrative medium, it's still coming into its own; there is a tremendous amount of possibility there that hasn't even begun to be realized. We still don't even really know what games *are*. I find the art vs. entertainment in gaming argument fantastically boring at this point, but I *am* interested in the narrative possibilities once we let go of whether or not a thing counts as art. What I think presents the greatest arena of possibility, the thing that sets games apart from all other storytelling media, is that aspect of player choice. But I don't think we understand what that choice means or where it really is. Choice is like consent: it's a state and an ongoing process, not a singular moment in time. Even in games where our options are severely constrained by design, we still make the choice to be there, to perform the actions regarding which we supposedly have no choice.

I think it's yet another mark of the continuing ambivalence around the legitimacy of digital forms of technology that we still regard things like games as facile locations for narrative construction; it's certainly not the only aspect of that attitude, but it's a major one. Technology is ruining stories, technology is ruining the novel, technology is making us all stupid and distractible and technology isn't worth writing about anyway. But we all make choices in stories. We're all complicit in the telling, the experiencing. What video games make possible is the confrontation of the meaning of that complicity. They make it possible to examine why we make those choices, over and over. Why we keep walking.

What *The Line* wants you to understand is that when you examine that, you may not like what you see. But it doesn't want you to look away.

It's been over a year, and I still can't. But I just started playing *The Line* again last week.

I'm still walking.

Player vs Game: Design, narrative, and power

(as Sarah Wanenchak)

Of all the games that comment on themselves – and it seems like there are more and more of those – I won't say that The Stanley Parable is the best, but I definitely haven't played another that made its intentions more blatantly clear or went for what it was after so aggressively. *The Stanley Parable*, originally a *Half Life 2* mod, has a lot to say about games. But I think it also has a lot to say about everything.

Essentially, *The Stanley Parable* is the story of a man named Stanley (surprise), a mundane office worker in a mundane, soul-killing job that involves sitting at a computer terminal and pressing the buttons he's told to press. One day, Stanley looks up from his desk to find all his co-workers gone and his office deserted. Confused and more than a little concerned (the narrator tells us), Stanley takes the outrageously courageous step of getting up and sallying forth to discover what exactly is going on.

At this point the player has a choice (in a sense). They

can follow the pre-conceived script, delivered to them via instructions from the narrator framed as simple narration of Stanley's actions. If they do this, they'll encounter a mind-control facility hidden in the bowels of the building, which they will turn off, and emerge – free at last – into an idyllic, sun-drenched countryside. On the other hand, the player can disobey the narrator's instructions, and alternately find themselves in scenarios involving, among other things, a game that revolves around a baby and fire, a massive explosion, the total breakdown of the game itself, and a very erratic Stanley Parable Adventure Line™.

The game is obviously complex in terms of its critique, and is working on multiple levels. It can be understood as a skewering of Office Space-style labor, but also a criticism of the way narrative works in games to constrain player agency. The story of Stanley and the narrator is the story of a clash of wills, and when Stanley/the player refuses to go along with the narrator's directions, the narrator reacts with bemusement, shock, confusion, and anger – as well as a jaunty instructional video concerning the importance of making good choices.

The choice argument/discussion/thing in games has been going on for quite a while – a lot of games make selling points out of the fact that they offer so many choices, or a few meaningful choices, or multiple endings, or just giant sandboxes in which to play and murder people a la the *Grant Theft Auto* franchise. The thing is that choice in games is complicated by the relationship between rules and fiction, something on which *The Stanley Parable* also comments. If the game's object is essentially to lead a player through a pre-determined plot, then the player can't be allowed to deviate from the plot much, if at all, for fear of ruining the story – not just in the sense of the events of the plot itself, but in the sense of narrative flow. For instance, if the plot's sense of urgency requires you to rush from point A to point B to prevent a character from being beheaded, taking your time to explore a few hallways and scavenge around for items diminishes that sense a bit.

In other words, a fiction-focused game is going to be very constraining in terms of its rules – the logic of the gameworld won't allow the player very much in the way of meaningful action outside of what they're "supposed" to be doing (I realize that there are a few exceptions to this, but I'm purposefully speaking in somewhat problematic generalities here). These games can be understood as *progressive*, while games that focus on rules and play without much emphasis on story are *emergent*. The former doesn't allow the player much agency, and the game will proceed in pretty much the same fashion each time. The latter presents the possibility of huge variance in the way each game might go – the rules are established, and then the player is free to play the game in whatever way they would like, within those established rules. Emergent games don't require stories at all, but progressive games do require rules. As Jesper Juul says, "Though rules can function independent of fiction, fiction depends on rules".[44]

This isn't just true of games, it's true of everything. Every story of any kind that we tell about anything at all depends on rules – in the sense of assumed conventions of what's appropriate and possible – to make itself coherent.

One of the elements of the whole choice debate in gaming is the question of whether choice/agency in games is necessarily a good thing all of the time. Some players expect and demand choices in the games they play, and judge the quality of a game according to whether or not meaningful choices are available.

The difference between choice in emergent versus progressive games isn't just about the sheer amount of choice that you have but about *meaning*. Choice in a narrative game has – if the game is done well – the emotional weight and resonance that participation in a powerful story should have. In my own personal experience, in fact, powerful narrative makes choice irrelevant. I get so caught up in the story being told that *I don't notice* the way the gameplay itself is constructed, nor do I care about it if I notice.

An example of this is *Enslaved: Odyssey to the West*, which featured decidedly lackluster gameplay; however, I couldn't have cared less because I was so enraptured by the story itself that the gameplay was simply a means to the next part of the story. I literally did not notice that I was really playing sort of a *meh* game. When I played *The Last of Us*, I had absolutely no say in anything that happened in the story – very little of what I did impacted anything related to the narrative at all. Again, I didn't notice, nor did I notice that the gameplay became a bit repetitive; all that mattered to me was the story.

So the story – and the construction and flow and assumptions of narrative – were actually obscuring elements of design. These elements may or may not have mattered, depending on what type of gamer I was, but still.

We need to ask whether agency is always a plus. I'm not sure if it is, in a game like *The Last of Us*. But we also need to understand what we mean by agency.

An essay written a few years back by Steven Poole on games and labor[45] questions whether the format of many contemporary games might not a problem. Poole suggests that games like *The Sims* and *Farmville* reproduce a normalized capitalist, wage-serf/data serf view of play, and therefore the world, and the ludic structure of these games forecloses on any possibility of meaningful resistance:

> Be loyal, keep your head down, earn currency. Nothing could be a more perfect advert for what is sometimes called the "American way" than *The Sims*. Buy a Sim a large mirror and she will be happier, by virtue of being able to gaze at her reflection. Buy him a new oven, and he'll become more popular after giving dinner parties. Help your Sim climb the slippery pole

of a career as a politician or scientist. This is a game in which the brutal rules of free-market capitalism are everything. More money makes a Sim happier; social dissidents are not allowed. Do you want to drop out of the rat-race, wear charity-shop tweed suits and spend your days playing chess in the park? Sorry. Such gameplay possibilities are ruled out by the political assumptions buried deep in the game's structure.

There's certainly something about the activities in these games that's somehow weirdly satisfying, even if they do replicate meaningless, repetitive jobs – why else would they be so popular? It shouldn't escape our attention that, though games like *Farmville* are certainly more emergent than progressive, they still rely on at least a basic narrative foundation that makes activity within the game meaningful. In *Farmville,* you're a farmer – very simple, but making explicit reference to narrative tropes of romantic simplicity and authenticity with which most of us are at least sort of familiar. In *World of Warcraft*, the mythos that backgrounds less story-oriented player action is Tolkienesque in its complexity and depth. In *The Sims,* the design of character interaction encourages players to construct their own narrative for the lives of their Sims – I know I used to create entire soap operas in my head around feeding babies and going to work and utterly failing to cook lobster.

Even in these games – again, more emergent than progressive – narrative plays a role, and an important one.

On the surface it appears to simply be making games potentially more involving, more "fun". But its secondary – and perhaps more important – function is to obscure the realities of the game's design. You don't really notice what it is that you're doing.

I've had more than one moment where I've looked up from one of these games and realized that I wasn't even really having *fun* anymore. And yet I had blown an entire hour on it.

So why does this matter, outside of games? Because it highlights one of the ways in which narratives and design work together toward ends that can be less than positive. The most powerful narratives that pattern our daily experience fade into the background of everything; they become so assumed that we never think to question them or wonder what it is that they're really doing. In a previous piece,[46] David Banks made some incredibly important points about how the assumptions behind certain kinds of design come about, proceeding from an alarming location of power and privilege. The design of our objects might appear to have nothing to do with narrative, but in fact narratives about what's good, right, and desirable provide a context for how the work of design is done. So narratives about an idealized – and *attainable* – middle class suburban/exurban lifestyle provide the context for a coffee machine whose light is way too bright.

If we don't ask questions about what narrative does, about *who it serves*, we miss that.

I love stories. I think they're one of the most worthwhile, important things that we do as a species. But that doesn't mean that stories are an absolute good, or that narratives are always pathways leading to a positive end. *Who tells stories* matters, as well as why they're told. Our narratives both constrain and are constrained by structures of power. If we don't sensitize ourselves to that, there are all kinds of things we won't see that we probably should.

Some Fragmentary Thoughts on

The Last of Us

I've made sporadic, clumsy attempts to write about video games on this blog before, and here's another. I do think I might do this more, though, because I write about games a good deal in a vaguely academic sense for *Cyborgology*, and when I do, I tend to come at them from a narrative-focused perspective, though I've also written about things like mechanics and game design (and DRM) because you can't really separate those things from narrative in a game – yeah, that pretty much tips my hand on where I come down in the now-tired ludology/narratology debate.

I also tend to be behind in terms of writing about games that you have to pay more than about $10 for. This is because so much of my time is taken up by writing and teaching and other related stuff, and also because, for financial reasons, I tend to really, really try to wait for Steam sales, which usually puts me a few months behind at least.

All that said, I got *The Last of Us* for Christmas and I have some Thoughts. Here they are.

- I'm both impressed and a little startled that something this much of a trope salad ends up not feeling like a game that's desperately and clumsily trying to please an audience that's already been pounded to death by post-apocalyptic militaristic zombie dystopias. I don't know if it's because of how emotionally engaging the story manages to be or whether I'm just still a sucker for things like *The Road,* but I never found the obviously tropey stuff distracting or clangy. It somehow all meshes together and feels of a piece. That's saying something about the quality of the writing involved.

- I cannot even believe the voice acting. This should be the standard that all other narrative-driven games try to meet, because you know? Voices mean a lot. They might mean just about everything. Facial animation helps, but man.

- Boy, a lot of the first half of it reminded me of *Enslaved.* I fucking loved that game.

- I do largely agree with Christopher Franklin[47] that the game is working within a limited design format that ends up creating a slightly jarring disconnect between cutscenes and combat. *The Last of Us* is clearly trying to connect the two in a way that feels meaningful, but it doesn't quite stick the landing. In what is – in my opinion – an otherwise nearly perfect game, that's the one really noticeable false note.

- I loved the ending. I see why some people seem to not have done. But for me, the emptiness and the bleakness fit the rest of the game's mood. I also found the ambiguity about the future more satisfying than I think others did. No, there are no immediate consequences for the choice that gets made. But I think the game is strongly implying that there will be, and they won't be pretty. I like that the writers had the guts to leave the part to my imagination.

- Along those lines, I think the last game I played that was this emotionally brutal – aside from *The Walking Dead,* which also shares a lot of similarities here – was *Spec Ops: The Line,* though of course *The Last of Us* is nowhere near as overtly abusive. There were things that happened that literally had me staring at the screen in shock. There were things that made me say, out loud, "Oh my *God.*" There were things that I found deeply upsetting. Part of this is that I often lose myself in a story to the point where I don't clue into the parts that other people find predictable, but regardless. Like *The Line,* this is not a "fun" game. It's not trying to be.

- Further along those lines, probably what I found bravest and most effective is something else that the game shares in common with *The Line*, which is a deep skepticism about the idea of heroes in games wherein the protagonist commits acts of horrendous, cruel violence. Walt Williams, the lead writer for *The Line*, said in an interview something that I love and has stayed with me: "Your main character can never be more righteous than the core mechanic demands." In other words, *don't do or be Nathan Drake*. If you're killing hundreds and even thousands of people, you are or must become a mutilated monster of a human being in some very fundamental ways, and the game's story – if there is one – needs to address that in some way. *Uncharted* does not. *The Last of Us* does. Joel is not a hero. Joel is an emotionally ruined selfish wreck of a human being and he makes horrible choices. When the game ends and you sit there feeling sad and empty, I think that's pretty much how you should feel.

- *Even further* along those lines, I think *The Last of Us* does something else that makes the characterization of Joel even more poignant and effective: it makes it very, very clear that most of the people Joel/you kill aren't special or evil or even significantly different than Joel himself. Almost everyone in the game is simply doing whatever they perceive is necessary for their own survival. No one is a *good* person; the world doesn't allow them to be. As Joel says at one point, "it was either him or me."

This is something else that *The Line* attempted to do: to humanize the people you kill, to make it clear that they're just people, as lost and confused as the protagonist, desperately fighting to stay alive. That said, the one way in which this fails – and also failed in *The Line,* though I think you could also argue that it's part of Martin Walker's crazed attempt to justify to himself what he's done – is that no one is really ever afraid of you, at least not in the gameplay segments. They remark on how startling and worrying it is that you've killed so many of their friends, but no one cowers in corners and pleads for you to spare their lives, unless they then attack you seconds later. No one runs in terror or tries to shield their friends from your bullets. They just come at you, over and over and over in a human wave, and you kill them. In that, the game both humanizes *and* dehumanizes them, and not in the conscious way in which *The Line* worked. It's another slightly false note, though on my first playthrough I didn't notice that it detracted from the experience at all. And in fact, I suspect that that has more to do with how accustomed I am to playing a game like that than the quality of the game itself.

I'm not sure how to fix this, and I'm skeptical that actually having NPC enemies *do* those things would be fully effective. I think the problem is, yet again, core mechanics, the fact that in a game like this, killing – even lent emotional weight by the narrative – is fundamentally problem-solving, something that has to be done in order to allow you to move through to the next cutscene. Again, I think *The Line* was aware of this and managed to make some narrative use of it, but it didn't seem to me as though *The Last of Us* was, and I'm not sure how it could have been that kind of self-aware without being an entirely different kind of game.

A game that *does* do this – that does almost everything that *The Last of Us* is trying to do and does it much better – is *The Walking Dead*, but that game makes use of different mechanics; I think that's a huge part of why it's able to do these things more effectively. So again we're simply running up against the inherent limitations of a particular kind of game.

Again, for what it is, I regard *The Last of Us* as a game that comes about as close to perfect as a game like itself could. It's definitely on my list of the top ten games I've ever played. But again, I'm with Christopher Franklin in seeing it as also a perfect example of what this kind of game really just *can't do*, at least not as it currently stands. I think it also stands as a call for something better, for something new in terms of how we blend mechanics with storytelling. So I'm optimistic about what *The Last of Us* means and is doing.

And I'm playing it all again, so that definitely has to mean something.

No More Princesses, No More Castles

Note: Here follow major spoilers.

I'm not sure when, in the course of playing *The Last of Us: Left Behind,* I actually started laughing aloud in delight. It couldn't have been all that early on. When I think about it, I think it might actually have been the minigames – and I can't even bear to call them minigames because they weren't that at all. They were games, yes, but they were games that I was playing with my friend, and they were games that I was helping Ellie play with her friend, and the two blended together and the "minigames" became a desperately joyful grab for the last vestiges of childhood. Throwing bricks at car windows. Messing around in a photo booth. Playing in an arcade. Trying on Halloween masks. These didn't feel like tacked-on activities designed to bloat the content. They felt real, vital. I was laughing as I played them, and for a few minutes, laughing, I managed to forget about the end I knew was coming.

~

One of the worst ideas to come along in gaming is that we somehow need to make games *for* "girls". As if anyone who isn't a (usually white) straight, cisgender man needs something carefully and prettily packaged and handed over with such delicacy, so that neither it nor the recipient breaks. *Here,* here is *your* game. The rest of us will go on with ours.

What a poisonous fucking concept. Honestly.

~

The Last of Us was remarkable to me right from the start, for most of the reasons that it was remarkable to everyone else – the graphics, the worldbuilding, the writing, the characters, the voice acting, the music (oh, *God*, the music), the story, the genuine tension that infuses so much of the combat. But what was truly remarkable to me was Ellie. She's a girl, but she's no princess in a castle, nor is she placed in danger merely to motivate the (male) main character. As Joel – who has already lost one daughter – you naturally want to protect her, and saving her is indeed his primary motivation in the end. But this motivation is presented with its legitimacy in a state of crisis. Joel is an emotionally mutilated, ultimately profoundly selfish person. When he sacrifices everything – *everything* – to save Ellie, the game doesn't present this as just another example in a long line of princesses in castles. It's left open to question whether Ellie would have needed or wanted saving.

And Ellie saves Joel. More than once. More than once, he would literally be dead without her.

More than that, Ellie isn't a motivator. Ellie is *real*. She sings and tells bad jokes and gets really sarcastic and yells when you make mistakes and kills when she has to and reacts with horror when you kill. She has memories, desires, motivations of her own. When Joel wants to give up, Ellie demands that they continue, not so that his sacrifices will mean something but so that *hers* will. Ellie is a person, not a MacGuffin, and as a female character in that role she puts both of the later entries into the *Bioshock* franchise – which I do love – to utter shame.

And you can *play* as her. You can play as her and the parts where you do are among the most terrifying, visceral, gripping parts of the game. They're not toss-ins. They're not there just for the sake of some gameplay variety. They're there because *Ellie is a person and the game is treating her like one.*

The Last of Us was by no means the first excellent game I'd gone through where a primary female character was playable, but there was something about it that felt different, deeper, more real. I was being invited to consider Ellie. I was being invited to see something differently than I was used to.

~

"Forty-seven percent of all game players are women. In fact, women over the age of 18 represent a significantly greater portion of the game-playing population (30 percent) than boys age 17 or younger (18 percent)." –

Sunny Moraine

Entertainment Software Association, 2013.[48]

~

The fact that you go into *Left Behind* knowing how the story of Ellie and Riley ends does nothing to make it less of an experience. If anything, it makes it more of one. Every happy moment, every minute of conflict, every second together – you're trying to stretch it out, trying to make it last, as if you're Ellie herself and you're looking back on this final stretch of a few hours in the lives of these two girls, looking and willing it not to end and knowing that it will. Every part stabs home.

I loved Riley because I knew I was about to lose her, though I would have loved her anyway, because no part of the game in which she appears feels wasted. Her character is revealed in a thousand little ways, from her fabulously well-animated facial expressions to her inability to talk to Ellie about her deeper feelings to her insistence that they capture a few last fragments of their childhood together. Like Ellie, she doesn't feel like a throwaway element to make the player more "emotionally invested". She's there because she's real and necessary. Everything Naughty Dog does to make her that way isn't just so you'll grieve the loss of her. It's so you'll love her the way Ellie does, and you'll regard her memory as something precious.

Naughty Dog does this in a way I've seen few other games dare to do: it does it gently. It doesn't drag you in; it simply opens a path for you. It seems to trust you to find your own way.

~

I remember reading about the kerfuffle that apparently happened around the simple placement of Ellie on the box art for *The Last of Us*[49] – that is to say, in the foreground. Ashley Johnson, the actress who gave Ellie her voice, had some opinions about it:

> I feel like they don't put women on the covers because they're afraid that it won't sell. It's all gamers really know—and I don't want to be sexist by any means—but I get the feeling, generally, that they think games won't sell as well with a woman on the cover, compared to some badass dude on the front.

I can't help feeling that she's right. I *know* that she's right. There are exceptions, of course, but they're exceptions precisely because they're exceptional. For the most part, this is what we get. If there's a secondary female character, she's pushed to the side, often in a pose that suggests vulnerability, and of those times, all too often she's hanging off the male character in worried adoration. This is what marketing departments think we want. And until something changes, until companies finally say no, it will indeed continue to be what we expect.

Naughty Dog said no.

In order for a mass demand for something different to exist, we need to be able to imagine that something different as something possible.

~

The kiss between Riley and Ellie was something I completely expected and at the same time never believed would really happen. I had felt it building, I had sensed that things were edging in that direction, but I was constantly second-guessing it as I played. *I probably just have the slash goggles on. It's wishful thinking. Maybe they're teasing the possibility as a way of tossing people like me a bone, but it won't happen. They wouldn't have the guts. Sad, because they're so brave in other respects, but probably true.*

Then it happened. I'm not sure what I did. I think I may have cheered aloud; I think I might have pumped my fist in the air. It felt like more than a bone-toss; it felt like a great big welcoming hug, an acknowledgment of humanity, and even more, it felt like a victory, like something that had been fought for. Because it had.

Positive depictions of queer characters in games are no longer an impossibility, but like women on the box art, they're still remarkable exceptions, and wherever they appear you get the petulant whining of people who are threatened by anything outside of what they find comfortable and familiar. So it didn't surprise me at all to find out that the same thing happened here. But more than that, I was distressed by some of the other, more insidious things people were saying: *They're just kids so it can't be real, they're just confused, it was just put in there for shock value.*

Just. Seriously? Ask queer kids when they knew they were queer, or at least when they began to strongly suspect. Tally up the answers. And then shut your goddamn mouth.

~

It continues to escape me why so many adult consumers of entertainment content are so terrified of being treated like adults.

But it does help to explain why so many producers of entertainment content refuse to treat them like they are.

~

The thing is, as a friend of mine said, *it doesn't even really matter why* Naughty Dog made that creative decision – though I refuse to believe it was last-minute, given how effortlessly it works with Ellie's character in the main game, as well as the history with Riley at which she hints. What matters is how I – and so many others – felt, which was elated, recognized, valued. I often forget how dehumanized I end up being made to feel when I play video games, even games I love – *Dishonored,* and *Bioshock Infinite,* to name two recent examples – and I forget that I feel that way *because I am just that used to it*. It's a feature of my landscape. So to find a game that doesn't make me feel that way is utter joy.

I shouldn't ignore another game that made me feel

that kind of bittersweet joy: *Gone Home,* which stands as one of my top games of 2013. I felt the same creeping hope when I sensed the direction in which the story might be going, and I felt the same elation when that hope proved justified. But *Gone Home* is an independent game, and as such it enjoys a degree of freedom that a game from a studio as big as Naughty Dog is might not. People expect indie games to take risks and push boundaries – that's one reason why we love them. But mainstream titles are the status quo, and they're supposed to maintain it. That's what we expect them to do. So what Naughty Dog decided to do *did* shock me, because I didn't see it coming from them. And it made me all the more happy for it. If it was inserted for shock value, it worked.

~

Left Behind isn't by any means perfect. Parts of it feel disjointed, and the combat feels almost as if it was inserted because it was indeed something people expected – not a problem for me, because I enjoyed *The Last of Us*'s combat, but it still didn't quite mesh. But the high points are so high that I don't care; perfection or the lack of it doesn't really matter, because it's not the point. Naughty Dog presented me with two girls whom it clearly feels have the right to exist on their own terms, to fight and be afraid and be angry and be strong and be weak, and to love and be loved. I might be waxing overly rhapsodic here, but I can't overstate how much this meant to me personally. A big-budget mainstream game treated me like a human being.

That happens so terribly rarely.

Ellie and Riley are more than amazing people in an amazing story. They're a challenge.

Let's see who's brave enough to answer.

Sunny Moraine

On Tech

Sunny Moraine

Autobiography Through Devices

(as Sarah Wanenchak)

In order to understand my relationship with computers, you need to understand that I have terrible handwriting.

Do not try to tell me that yours is worse. It isn't. I promise. My bad handwriting is a combination of a number of different things both contemporary and historical, including an inability to hold a writing implement in a way that even approaches comfortable, impatience, the fact that I literally never learned to form letters "correctly", and probably some neurological stuff that goes formally undiagnosed. I don't just write illegibly, I write *illiterately*: I skip letters, I place them out of order in words, I can't space or block sentences. I completely abandon rhyme or reason when it comes to capitalization (my punctuation is impeccable, though). I'm not dyslexic, not that we've ever been able to determine, though again, there probably *is* something going on there. I just… can't write by hand. At all.

And I'm a writer.

More, I'm a writer because of computers. I can't

emphasize this enough: Without digital technology, *I would not be a writer,* at least not the way I am now. I've written before that computers gave me my words. That's true. That's the backbone of this, the place from which we have to start. Everything else proceeds from there.

~

The first computer – the first digital *anything* – that I remember was my father's little Kaypro. I loved that thing. I loved everything about it. I don't remember when or how it entered the house, or if it was just always there, but I remember how big it seemed, how bright the green characters on the black display were, the sound of the keyboard, the louder and vaguely alarming rattly sound of the printer. I gave them names: They were Puter and Ticky.

I also used them. It started very early. Going by some old photos I have, I couldn't have been more than one.

The thing is, for a long time the idea that I could use the keyboard to assemble the various letters into coherent sentences was alien to me; I knew it was possible, I just had no idea how to go about doing it and didn't yet feel a need to learn. What I *did* do was repeatedly mash my hands on the keyboard and then force my father to print out the resulting gibberish and read it aloud to me. I laughed. Oh, how I laughed and laughed. It was a simpler time.

A Brief History of the Future

Then, much later, we got the Apple IIci.

Now this was quite exciting. There was color! There was a GUI! AND. There were *games*. I'd played games before at school – there was *Odell Lake* and a few other things I can't remember, though I don't think I came to *Oregon Trail* until a while later – but these games were complicated and colorful and *weird* and had involved stories and were so, so exciting. I should note at this point that I never had a game console or indeed a TV – growing up, though I did hang out with friends who did. But I never played. Until the computer.

~

This is the other thing you have to understand. For me, digital technology is about friends, about work, about connection, about entertainment, about research, about sex, about identity, about fandom, about politics, about all the stuff that it's about for most people in various different combinations. But for me what it's *really* about, besides words, is play. Play came before the words. In fact, if I'm being honest, play is part of what made the words themselves possible.

These weren't just pixels. These were worlds. I'd spent years creating other universes in my head; now here they were in front of me, and so what if they were small and grainy and *at best* rendered in 256 colors? For a lot of kids my age it was no big deal. For me it was a revelation, and I had no idea – sitting there and playing the demo of a

knockoff Star Trek game with a keyboard and trackball –
the degree to which it would shape my life for decades
after.

~

What really changed everything, I think, was *Myst*.

A lot of people don't remember *Myst* anymore. Which
is strange, because when it was released it was hailed as a
new chapter in computer games, something that would
forever alter what we thought was possible in the genre(s)
and what could be done with the medium. *Myst's* genre –
point-and-click adventure – hasn't died, but it's definitely
become a niche genre rather than the juggernaut that
people were predicting. Nevertheless, for me it really was
that kind of watershed moment.

Myst looks incredibly dated now – its pre-rendered
background screens are static for the most part and clumsy
to the eye. What movement there is consists of grainy in-
screen Quicktime films. Yet it was amazing to me, a game
that was fundamentally about an atmosphere and a sense
of place, a space in which the entire point was to explore. It
was also a *safe* space, where death was impossible, that
nevertheless contained a definite sense of unease. It was
made to feel open but was actually quite linear, plotted out
beforehand, though there were several possible endings.
One of them, the "best" one, led to the player being given
Myst island and the freedom to return to it whenever they
wanted. After I finished the game, I found myself booting

it up many times after, simply to wander around and be in that place.

I think it was that open space that made me realize that I could create within it. I could fill this digital space with my own stories. A lot of people have regarded video/computer games as things that have made an entire generation imaginatively lazy; for me it was an explosion of imagination. These were tools that I could make use of, an imaginative space that I could use as raw material for the creation of my own fictions. Much later came consoles, came *Half Life* and *Portal* and *Enslaved* and *Journey* and *The Last of Us* and *Bioshock* and *Spec Ops: The Line* and *The Walking Dead* (point-and-click, appropriately), but I owe my entry into that world to a little pre-rendered window on my dad's Apple IIci and a few crappy minutes of live-action footage.

~

But the last piece slotting into place was the internet.

I think I first recall using the internet with – as usual – the assistance of my father, who had gotten a home connection for work – like so many of us, the sound of a dial-up connection stirs deep memories in me. I didn't immediately discover actual real-time interaction with other human beings until a good bit later, though I was vaguely aware of chatrooms. What I discovered was fandom – mostly fan sites for movies and TV that I loved (by then I had regular access to television), most particularly *Star Wars* and later on *The X Files*.

Star Wars was my first experience of fanfiction – in middle school – and I distinctly remember being confused about whether or not these works of fiction were actually canon in some way. What I first came upon was – of course – fairly sexually explicit, and I remember being both intrigued and vaguely troubled by that. But I was hooked. I soon gained an understanding of what exactly I was seeing and devoured whatever I could find. It was yet another moment of revelation. *People* could write fiction about the stuff they loved and share it with others. Not *authors* but just people.

People like me. And at last, a method of writing that for years had been awkward and painful was no longer an obstacle.

Right around this time I met someone who would remain my closest friend all through high school, though we later had a falling-out from which we haven't recovered. *She* had AOL, and it was there that I discovered AIM, other fans, other friends who I had never met and might never meet, but as a weird, lonely kid in school, the sudden ability to make contact with a world of other people like me was intensely liberating.

At this person's house were also *yet more games* – *Zork Nemesis, Zork: Grand Inquisitor,* and some of my first exposure to shooters in the forms of *Rainbow Six, Quake* and *Soldier of Fortune.* This was something else: games could be *violent,* and that wasn't frightening to me but rather massively exciting (I had seen games like *Mortal Kombat* and *Doom,* but had only had limited contact with them). I now realize that, among other things, I was very angry during that time; here was an outlet for that anger.

High school was marked by an even deeper immersion into fandom and the friends I found there, partly as a result of the emotional difficulties I had in a transition from a small private middle school to a public high school that contained, as I recall, about a thousand students to a class. Life was not fun. Fantasy was an escape, and while I had made some clumsy attempts at fanfiction before, now I took to it with a kind of desperation. I could write things, and other people would like them. There was instant ego-propping-up-of. I think my parents were troubled by this – we now had a fancy new iMac and I was spending a huge amount of time on it – but at the time I insisted that I needed what I was getting from it and I maintain that that was largely true. It wasn't indulgence; it was a survival mechanism. Digital technology, at that point, was a lifeline.

It was also play with identity in a sense that I had never done before. I discovered fandom roleplay, a perfect analog to the pretending I had done as a child. I could write and perform in digital space as other people. I could lose myself in that, try on different things, see how well they fit with my understanding of who my adolescent self was becoming.

I met my now-husband through the internet, via a comment on a message board about looking for other local fans of a band I was into. He contacted me. We became friends, and then more than friends.

Then the internet went away for a while.

After high school I "took a year off", which turned into two years, which turned into relative poverty and a string of awful retail and temp jobs. During that time, I had an old PowerMac in my one-room apartment, but I had no connection to what I had come to understand as the larger outside world, and it was deeply isolating. After a year or so of this, I managed to get a cheap dial-up line, and that was better. Two years or so after moving out of my parents' house I finally started college, which gave me access to on-campus computers and a faster internet connection – now I had LiveJournal and AIM and fandom again, and it was a profound relief, a sense of recovering a deep part of myself that I had lost for a while.

Right around this time, I also (finally) got a cell phone, a dinky little flip phone that I probably still have in a drawer somewhere. I could dial a number and that was it. But it was still a remarkable feeling, being able to call someone at any time, anywhere I wanted.

(You might notice that I haven't said much about cell phones in this piece and I don't intend to; they've never played that big a role for me in terms of forming who I am or shaping my day-to-day existence. I've never owned a smartphone and I still don't. My experiences with digital technology have been almost entirely focused around desktop computers, laptops, and now tablets.)

This is the thing about me and digital technology, which I think holds true for so many of us: What too many people still talk about – and what I think my parents saw then – as disconnection was, for me, connection of the most profound kind. Yes, it was all a sort of escapism, but it was also a tether to the things that made life emotionally bearable. That's no longer *as* true – I don't need everything I find here to stay sane – but it's still where I'm creative, where I make friends, where I play. It's so much a part of who I am as a person, of how I understand myself, that I can't imagine myself apart from it. I wouldn't *want* to.

This makes me realize something else about the people who talk about digital technology in terms of *disconnection* and who puff themselves up about eschewing it: Access to it is a privilege, but being able to choose to push it aside is a kind of privilege too. It denies the experiences of those of us who really *benefit* from it, for whom it represents liberation. Those of us who are socially awkward, queer in deeply queer-unfriendly spaces, disabled, isolated, questioning everything we are, questioning everything *period*.

It can't mean the same thing to every person. This is what it's meant for me.

Sunny Moraine

Dispatches from Ephemeral Social Media

(as Sarah Wanenchak)

You don't have to prove that you were there, that it happened, that it mattered, because it doesn't, because it isn't worthy of record, because nothing is. You capture an instant of it, a series of seconds. You shoot it out into the ether. Some people see it. You'll never know how it affected them. You'll never think it matters.

Here is you laughing with a forty in your hand, or – when you're younger and less concerned with appearances, or maybe *more* concerned with appearances but less skilled in managing them according to what's likely to be well-received – a wine cooler. It's probably the height of irony that you care about appearances when it will be gone in a matter of seconds, but we're humans and this is what we do. Either way you don't have to worry. You, half-clothed in the middle of a street glittering with shattered glass, waving your arms into the streetlights. You, making out with a stranger in a fit of ill-advised exuberance; who cares who's doing the advising, anyway? No one says YOLO anymore, no one remembers what YOLO meant, but the concept applies.

A Brief History of the Future

You pick life apart one second at a time; it's not a net or a book of records or a server farm full of bytes and bits but grains of sand that slip through yours and everyone's fingers. You feel the texture of each one as it passes over your skin. Your nerves document each one in flashes of sensory input. Then it's gone and you never miss it again.

~

There are several ways you can do this.

You can flash-capture, flash-send, and it's gone when you send it, and it's gone when they see it. These are moments of incredible intimacy, and to the degree that you've chosen someone to whom it matters at all, they devour the image or the words, they burn it into their memories, and then the object is gone but the memories might remain. I say *might* because we all know that memories are fickle, but they can also be startlingly robust.

You may be on your deathbed two thirds of a century later and out of nowhere you'll remember when your boyfriend sent you a picture of his dick with a ribbon wrapped around it for your birthday and you'll laugh and become wistful because it was actually a very sweet gesture at the time.

You'll remember when that girl you spent one night with in San Francisco with wine and tears in the rain sent you, months later, the message that she loved you, and you know she never saw it again, and you never saw it again, and you never saw *her* again but it's there. Somewhere. It's hard to say.

Sometimes in the intervening years between when it happened and when it might make its final deathbed appearance you wish that someone somewhere kept it. Maybe someone somewhere did. Somehow.

~

Or:

You can send it out like you're tossing rice at a wedding where you don't care about anyone, especially not the people getting married. You can scatter it all over and deny that it matters at all. The second you hit *post* it's gone from the thing you used to send it, and as soon as anyone sees it it's gone from their feed. There are ways to counter this, there are apps and hacks, but no one does this in the kind of critical mass where anyone really cares. Everyone likes the freedom. Everyone likes not caring, and people don't unless you force them to.

So feeds are full of fragments of close friends and strangers, little iridium flares of information, there for a few seconds and gone again. Watch your feed for long enough and get a sense of the quality of rushing flow, of Not Stopping. All the delineated moments of people's lives and feelings and thoughts and creative expressions, all blended into a seamless running whole of a narrative. It's dizzying. Some people sit and stare at it for hours. It's all about forgetting. Maybe people want to forget themselves. Maybe people want the freedom to remember.

~

Destruction has always been a component of art, a running theme even in the fight against time and decay. Sometimes things double back and embrace it. In London a performance artist documents the first two years of the life of her first child in snippets of video that are gone seconds after they're taken. It would be a bold statement about something or other except at this point no one thinks it's strange.

~

No one thinks about the past anymore. No one focuses on ruins because everything's in ruins all the time. The experience of time is the experience of ruin. You don't have to look back. You also don't have to look forward, if nothing right now lasts. It'll all be gone. None of it matters except all of it does. Drink up. Someone else might get to it before you do and we can't have that. But there's more than enough for everyone and everyone's guaranteed their share.

~

The thing is that someone probably *is* saving all of it. We talk about it now and then, and some of us are morbidly obsessed with it. Someone keeping everything else while the rest of us let it all go. Someone is tracking us, someone is marking the shadows of ourselves as we move through the world, as we grow up like pencil-height on a doorframe. Like a parent, except they probably aren't proud of us. It's hard to be proud of something that isn't a person so much as a collection of data points.

So okay, yeah, that's probably happening. But they aren't going to pull up the aforementioned picture of the aforementioned forty being drunk when we have our first job interview after college, so who cares, really?

They just want to sell us things. Isn't this correct? And most of us are looking to buy, or are at least so used to it by now that it barely registers.

~

The older generation likes to complain about this. They have hard drives and they look through them like old photo albums. They wax nostalgic and it's sort of embarrassing. They show your friends baby photos – can you imagine, *baby photos* – and everyone is supposed to respond appropriately. But *appropriate* is changing. Like the generation before them, they're getting stuck in the past, too rooted, and while they resist the current the rest of us are flowing downstream.

They talk about when people had to be careful, or at least told themselves and each other that they had to be, and everyone talked about everything that happened for days after the fact and life was an endlessly looping six seconds of disaster.

It sounds awful, frankly. We still have the loops but they vanish under the piles of other loops that are in a state of constant self-destruct. Screw it, don't worry about it. Life is as it comes. Let them keep their bizarre simplistic ideas of privacy and their terror of forgetfulness as their brains begin to disintegrate.

Life without a trace seems possible. In our best moments we tell ourselves we might be free.

Sunny Moraine

Tempus Snapchats

(as Sarah Wanenchak)

A number of good pieces on Snapchat have already been written, at *Cyborgology* and other places, and I think there's a lot yet to talk about. I'm jumping on the bandwagon today because I think I see a conceptual area that's already been touched on that offers additional room for expansion.

Much has been made of Snapchat's inherent ephemerality, of the fact that its images are destroyed potentially seconds after they're captured, that nothing is saved or made even semi-permanent. Jeremy Antley has noted[50] that this introduces the possibility for different varieties of expression through technology, for changes to how we use social media for truth-telling. Nathan Jurgenson takes the ephemerality of Snapchat a step further[51] and argues that just as photographs have traditionally been understood to capture a piece of the present and transport it into the future, the kinds of temporary photography that we see in Snapchat do pretty much the opposite, and that, moreover, we can understand this as a kind of reaction to the sort of documentation that social media has historically encouraged:

[A]s we have seen, there is meaning in witnessing ephemerality itself, an appreciation of impermanence for its own sake. By carving a space away from the growing necessity to record and collect life into database museums, temporary photography encourages an appreciation of the importance of experiencing the present for its own sake.

In other words, temporary photography is doing something very interesting with *time*, and with our experience of the same. If we've traditionally understood photographs to be a fragment of the present experienced in the future, temporary photos are fragments of the present *experienced as the present*. The whole project of documentation is potentially thrown up for grabs.

To turn back to how photos have traditionally worked, I think this element of *temporal transport* is important to bear in mind before I go further. Photographs – indeed, I think all forms of documentation – are the technological means by which we capture elements of our present experience and remove them from what we experience as the linear timestream. This means that, as I've written before,[52] photographs are fundamentally both *time-laden* and *atemporal*.

When I wrote that, I was also writing about ruined space, about the very contemplation of ruin. At this point it's also important to note that ruin, at least for my purposes here, needn't and shouldn't be understood as confined to physical space. Documentation itself is always in a potential state of ruin,[53] even as we imbue it with a – often illusory – element of permanence, or at least with the idea of significant future age. But different kinds of documentation have different relationships with ruin, and sometimes the ruin is the point, and sometimes it isn't. Buddhist sand mandalas are created specifically to be destroyed, coupling a long and painstaking process of creation with a deep sense of the transience of all life. The process of making them is in itself a *memento mori*, a meditation on death. To return to photography, Susan Sontag put it beautifully when she argued that all photography was, in one way or another, about creating *mementos mori*:

> To take a photograph is to participate in another person's (or thing's) mortality, vulnerability, mutability. Precisely by slicing out this moment and freezing it, all photographs testify to time's relentless melt.
> —On Photography *(1973)*

But the process of making these time-slices atemporal is just that: a process. And the result exists for a stretch of time, enough time that it can be meditated upon. They don't simulate the experience of time flashing by us, or of us traveling forward through time at breathless speeds. They slow everything down, inviting us to pause and consider. Even ruin/decay art is about process, often slow process.

Snapchat has no process. At least not in that sense. The image's destruction is instantaneous. There's nothing to pause over. It's there and then gone. *Blink.*

In short, what I'm arguing here is that temporary photography in general – and Snapchat in particular – is not only a reaction to traditional forms of social media self-presentation, not only a twist on where and how we place our trust,[54] not only a twist on the abundance of documentation, but is a rethinking of what photography itself is and does, and, by extension, a rethinking of how we locate documentation within our experience of linear and alinear time. Photos have been atemporal; temporary photos are, by virtue of their emphemerality, deeply *temporal*. They're not removed from time; instead they're solidly located within it. They're the present remaining the present.

It would be easy, then, to think that this kind of photography is incapable of serving as a *memento mori*. As I said above, *mementos mori* have historically been artifacts with a long shelf life – architecture, photos, paintings, even clocks. They stick around. But I think temporary photography actually has the potential to serve as a new form of *memento mori*. Clocks that say *tempus fugit* on their faces aren't in themselves reminders of the fleeting nature of time. The passing seconds do that. There and then gone again, temporary and instantly destroyed photos – because they are so temporal – may provide an even clearer sense of just how fast the present slips away.

Unfortunately, as you probably already know, people

(as Sarah Wanenchak)

So, the whole @Horse_ebooks thing.

It's very soon after the fact, and I imagine that there will be a great deal of piercingly insightful analysis and commentary being written in the next few days about it all. This pretends to be neither insightful nor analysis, though I imagine it might be fair to call it commentary. A lot of what I've seen so far amounts to people's immediate emotional reactions to finding out that our favorite Twitter spambot wasn't a bot or all that legitimately spammy and I'm afraid that this is going to fall at least *sort of* into that category, because of where it starts.

A lot of people seem upset. My initial emotional reaction to the whole @Horse_ebooks thing? My pure, unconsidered, *genuine real non-digital lol* reaction? Delight. Utter delight.

Not like I'm so much cooler than *you*, person-out-there-who-is-upset; I just think our differing reactions are interesting, and are interesting in conjunction with what @Horse_ebooks was and is.

Here's why my predominant emotion regarding this matter is delight: Stories.

I've written what seems like books' worth of words on stories on this blog, usually to argue that fiction is as useful a tool as "non"-fiction, as well as to question the distinction between the two in the first place. But behind all that verbiage is a kind of goofy, Sagan-esque enthusiasm for us as storytelling creatures, and the lengths to which we'll go to wring meaning out of the most objectively "meaningless" things. We require stories to make sense of anything, of our own existence, of the passage of time, of tragedy and agony and joy, of endings and beginnings – which all stories have and no story ever has. We're born and we start telling stories and when we fall into unconsciousness our brain tells itself more stories and then when we die people start telling stories about *that*.

On Twitter I called us "little sacs of walking pattern recognition algorithms" and I stand by that assessment. And that's *fantastic,* in every sense of the word.

I look at the negative reactions to what's happened with @Horse_ebooks and I can't get away from the idea that the source of a lot of the discomfort is discovering that the story doesn't mean what we thought it did – that, in fact, *we* weren't the ones deciding what it meant (by the way, I think we still were), and even that *we were unwitting parts of someone else's story.* As Robinson Meyer at The Atlantic says,[55] "We thought we were obliging a program, a thing which needs no obliging, whereas in fact we were falling for a plan."

I think that's an interesting turn of phrase, "falling for". As if we were duped. Which of course you could argue that people were; @Horse_ebooks wasn't what it (mostly, to most of us) seemed to be. But being duped usually involves an element of betrayal, of malicious intent.

Here's a thing that I think: That while we see patterns in the noise, half the time we know that's exactly what we're doing, and the fact that they're *our* patterns makes them more meaningful to us. It's the *process of seeing*, not just what's seen, that makes what we bring back from it so significant.

If @Horse_ebooks is noise, then what's found is special, meaningful, individual. If it isn't noise, that calls all of the meaning and its making into question.

What I find *especially* weird about this – aside from the general wonderful weirdness of attaching so much emotional meaning to a supposed spambot Twitter account – is that it's almost an inversion of the usual digital dualist thinking that we've catalogued here. Usually something *human*-created, *human*-generated, physical and intimate and person-to-person is what's real and legitimate. I saw more than one person talk about this in terms of whether or not a "machine" could generate "art". Yet in this case the discovery that there's really an intentional human behind it all is disillusioning, and meaning itself seems to be taking a hit.

The thing is, what we thought was "pure" machine has turned out to be *what it was all along:* not "pure" anything. Some combination of a person and a screen and a system of interface. The exact details of how those things have all come together varies, but the general equation is the same. As David Banks asked on Twitter: At what point do we say that @Horse_ebooks is or is not human?

I think that's what I find oddest about this whole flurry of reactions: The idea that we had a real thing, and it isn't what we thought it was, so now it's not a real thing anymore. The idea that there ever was a "real" thing to begin with. And the idea that, in order for *our* thing that we made to be real, there had to be some kind of correct understanding of the real thing that our thing came from. That now our thing is less real because we were wrong.

Look, man, I dunno. I don't know what's going to happen to us and @Horse_ebooks. I don't know if we're gonna be okay (probably); it's late as I write this and I've had some wine and I'm worried I might be wandering into word-vomit territory here. I just know that I look back on "everything happens so much" and "inside every dog there exists a perfect" and part of me still nods its head and goes *hey man yeah* and that hasn't gone away. Something that I thought probably worked a certain way doesn't seem to have worked that way; if anything, I'm just reminded of how incredible our brains are and their slightly melancholy tendency to put us in positions to be let down. But a million monkeys can make something amazing,[56] sure; *look at yourself.*

We'll always have SMELL SMELL SMELL GOOD NEW NEW NEW slice drink MATCH SPARKLER (thrown in air) STARS STARS STARS

Recognizing the Digital Uncanny

(as Sarah Wanenchak)

When news stories started popping up around the mysterious YouTube account Webdriver Torso, more than one person noted that the truth behind it would almost certainly turn out to be nowhere near as interesting as all the speculation about what that truth might be. More than one person suggested that it might be better if no one find out the truth at all, because mysteries are pleasurable, no matter how much we might think we want them to be solved.

A quick primer, for those who don't know (this has been going on for a while but only came to my attention in the last few weeks): Webdriver Torso features approximately 77,000 separate 10 second videos featuring cycling colors and tones. The purpose of these videos and their content *was* unknown, and of course, this being the web, there was a frantic search for explanations as well as frantic speculation about same.

The explanation – of course – turned out to be very mundane:

Isaul Vargas, a New York-based software tester,

spotted the videos in a post on BoingBoing and recognised them from an automation conference he had been at a year ago. They were being shown by a European firm that made streaming software for set-top boxes, the kit that sits under a TV and connects to services such as Sky or Netflix.

The company needed to be able to quickly and reliably upload digital video, a capability which it tested by uploading short, randomly generated snippets to its YouTube channel and running image-recognition software on it. "Considering the volume of videos and the fact they use YouTube, it tells me that this is a large company testing their video encoding software and measuring how Youtube compresses the videos," says Vargas.[57]

Cue disappointed sigh. But the explanation doesn't interest me so much as how people reacted to this account and what they saw in it.

Something that pops up again and again in these news stories is @Horse_ebooks, primarily – I think – because that's the easiest social media reference point for many people. What was great – and frustrating – about @Horse_ebooks was what it revealed about our fascination with perceived signals in the noise, with hidden meaning behind what seems random. It served as a reminder that we are, as I said in a post after the @Horse-ebooks outing, "little sacs of walking pattern recognition algorithms".

With @Horse_ebooks, though, we thought we had the answers. We thought we knew what was going on. We didn't. It wasn't just a bot, it had real intent and purpose, and it was not randomness, at least not completely. And that ended up being disappointing for a lot of followers, because the meaning we thought we had found for ourselves had been put there by actual people. Our story was not legitimate. It wasn't just that the explanation was mundane; we thought we already *had* the explanation, and it *was* mundane. The problem was that a lot of people felt lied to.

Webdriver Torso was and is something quite different, and I think we can analyze it using the concept of the uncanny. With some modifications.

The uncanny, as it's commonly used, refers to the "uncomfortably strange", things that are *almost* recognizable but which fall short in such a way as to make us feel disoriented and repulsed – as with robots who look just human enough to be majorly creepy. That latter definition isn't entirely useful when it comes to Webdriver Torso, because it doesn't make much room for attraction and fascination, which we tend to feel even for the most nightmare-fueling mysteries. Webdriver Torso is uncanny because it presents the possibility of a signal that we feel we *almost* understand, but that lack of understanding is discomfiting and even frightening, depending on the context. We recognize order. Chaos is bewildering and therefore scary. But the *hint*s of order lurking within chaos are uncomfortable on an entirely different level, because we can't understand and we desperately want to in a very instinctive way.

An additional useful and related concept is abjection – an object that has been removed from the familiar symbolic order and is therefore rendered strange and threatening. The difference here is that this kind of mystery hasn't been removed from anything. It comes from the outside unknown and is unknowable; we feel like it *should* fit somewhere but it doesn't. It doesn't upset the social order but rather the order by which we understand anything at all. Normal ways of understanding no longer apply.

Another example that shows up in a number of these news pieces – an example that I think is much more analogous – is that of numbers stations. The explanation for the weird sounds and voices carried by these shortwave signals seems to also be relatively mundane, though still pleasantly unsettling: they're probably coded signals being sent to various undercover agents in various countries, shortwave radio being quite appropriate to the task. But the codes themselves are just that kind of uncanny: hints of signal in the noise that tantalize and unsettle.

What makes this particular to contemporary forms of technologically-mediated communication is that we're especially *primed* to look for signals in that noise and therefore especially worried when we aren't quite able to grasp those signals. This obviously isn't confined to the web; radio seems to do the job just as well. There's also, I would argue, something specific about audio that lends itself to this kind of uncannyness. Couple audio with video/images, as in the case of Webdriver Torso, and you truly have something special.

We can also see fascination with this kind of uncanny mystery in certain Augmented Reality Games (ARGs). Much of the time we know what we're dealing with, but sometimes we only find out once we're pretty deep into it, and in any case the results can feature exactly that kind of spine-shiver that one gets from listening to numbers stations recordings late at night. I'll never forget how I felt when I saw the spectrogram image that someone pulled out out of the static at the end of one of the songs on the Nine Inch Nails album *Year Zero*, a giant black hand reaching down out of the sky.

So what differentiates the workings of our capacity for pattern recognition between things like @Horse_ebooks and Webdriver Torso is that mystery, that need to understand, and discomfort at the elusiveness of the signal. Of course the understanding is never as fun. But the discomfort, while it lasts, is something we treasure even as it keeps us up at night.

Sunny Moraine

My Breakup With Facebook: A reflection

(as Sarah Wanenchak)

(Note: As of the publication of this book, I am now more active on Facebook, though still in a limited capacity. Fancy.)

People keep trying to add me on Facebook. This raises some interesting issues. Most of them have to do with the fact that I'm not on Facebook.

Technically I do have a Facebook account. It's just not in my legal name — it's in the name of my writerly pseudonym, and I got it primarily so I could maintain a Facebook fan page, which I read in some blog or other was a good thing for an aspiring up-and-coming writerly person to have.

When I got my writerly Facebook account, I also did have an account under my legal name, and I was pretty active there. As with many users, I used it as a means to keep up with a lot of distant friends and family, as well as to engage in conversation and link-aggregation with people I know more locally. It was fun. I liked it. I got a lot out of it.

Then, about a year ago, I left.

The reasons behind that decision were myriad and complex; some of them had to do with changes to Facebook's interface with which I had aesthetic issues (yeah, it did mean that much to me[58]) while some of them had to do with other gut-level issues. But after having spent this long away from something that almost everyone else I know uses on a daily basis, I think there's an additional, more identity-based reason why I left: The name I used Facebook under just didn't really feel like *mine.* Not here. Which I realize might sound suspiciously digital-dualist, but bear with me.

I've been puttering around the internet since puberty. Like a lot of weird, misfit kids, the internet presented itself to me as a kind of social sanctuary: an odd appearance or obvious discomfort in physically co-present settings were suddenly no longer obstacles to meeting people and making friends, and I felt free to experiment with an incredibly liberating kind of identity-play. Gender, sexuality, my ideas of what was important and valuable to me — all of these things felt up for grabs in a way that they never had before. Moreover, for the first time I was talking to people as weird and misfitting as me, and we were getting along swimmingly.

I'm guessing that there's a better than even chance that whoever is reading this right now has experienced something like that moment, where you felt like some people online who had never "met" in the traditional sense got you better than pretty much everyone at school. Then you know what I'm talking about, and you know how formative that moment can be. (Maybe I just had an unusually pathetic high school experience, but I really don't think so.)

So this was — and is — profoundly empowering. *I know these people. They know me. We get each other. They accept me for who I really am.* And that last, that *who I really am* — that was and is my most powerful experience of the internet to date: building myself. Deciding who and what I'm going to be. This self isn't divorced from my non-digital self; they have each profoundly influenced the construction of each other.[59] So please understand that I'm not suggesting that I broke up with Facebook because I found these two identities somehow mutually exclusive — or even meaningfully separate. Because that's not what I'm saying at all.

What I'm saying — among other things — is that the idea of using my legal name online was and remains very strange to me. It feels like a kind of denial of identity.

Even with the fact that it now allows pseudonyms, Facebook has always been a "real name" kind of place, a digital space where the physical is profoundly present, and where people create and maintain social connections that are also created or maintained in physically co-present space. Work, school, family: these are all deeply interwoven into the very fabric of what Facebook is and was constructed to be. Facebook and other forms of social media like it are built to be extensions and augmentations of the physical world, not imaginative escapes from it.

And for me it was like a collision of worlds. It felt very subtly out of my control. Things weren't compartmentalized in the way I was used to. The truth is that on a purely instinctive level I never really felt *safe* on Facebook.

Another caveat: I'm not saying that identity play and management isn't possible in a setting like Facebook. I think a huge percentage of its users would disagree with that pretty strongly, and again, there is the fact that they allow pseudonyms. What I'm saying is that Facebook felt fundamentally *different* to me in how identity was treated and transacted, and I never did get used to it.

So, for that and many other reasons, I left.

At first it was almost an experiment: *let's see if this is really possible.* Then it became more of an experiment in seeing what it was really *like.* I remembered a life without Facebook, but it had been a while and my memory of it was sort of hazy. And then it became something that I wanted to try to maintain as long as I could — again, to see what would happen. I kept my writer account, but although I'm still accepting friend requests, I pretty much never use it for anything. It feels like cheating at this point. It still also feels extremely odd.

So what's it been like, living (mostly) without Facebook? Am I more connected? Less lonely? Are my relationships more meaningful? Are my experiences more significant when not reduced to a status update?

Okay, for starters, kind of not at all because even if I'm not on Facebook I'm pretty much everywhere else. Twitter, Tumblr... yeah.

But no. To all of those questions. If anything, living (mostly) without Facebook has left me feeling more profoundly *disconnected*, from both distant friends and family and from people I see all the time in my PhD program. I don't get to talk to my aunt in Texas with such ease and lack of effort; I don't see her posting about my cousins or my other aunts and uncles. I don't see what my sister posts about from college. I miss my spouse's exchanges with many of his family members. I don't see what my friends in Maryland and DC post about; I've missed some fairly big developments because of this, and only found out about them long after the fact. Sure, we meet face-to-face in the halls or for dinner or drinks, but there is still a second ongoing stream of discussion and interaction among them to which I'm simply not privy.

And given that I'm missing it, often I'm not even aware of exactly what I'm missing.

The idea that "opting out" has a cost isn't a new one on this blog and has been better written-about[60] and better theorized[61] than this piece can or intends to do. My point is that yeah, there is indeed a cost, and it does indeed come into play within one's own social group. And it's not necessarily a small one. It's larger than I expected when I first suspended my account, because I did not understand then what a significant part Facebook played in all aspects of my social world, distant and local alike. Perhaps on some level I assumed that my relationships could just continue independently of Facebook exactly as I imagined they had before — that, to draw on Jenny Davis's connections made in the post linked above, I could continue my interaction rituals without suffering the damage caused by exits from them and without the repair and maintenance that Facebook allows for.

And that isn't so.

Why don't my other social media presences allow for this same kind of repair and maintenance? Because I don't use them the same way I used Facebook. I use them very much like I used the internet from my earliest days on it: as half expression and half escape, slipperier and more fraught with fiction and roleplay than Facebook was. As I continue with what looks like it might actually become a career as a fiction writer, this is changing somewhat, but it's still more true than not. My use of social media in particular and the internet in general is now more removed from the rest of my social life than it was before. It is still augmented, but it's now more severely compartmentalized.

Do I miss Facebook? Yes and no; I miss what it allowed me to do, the ways in which it made me feel so connected. Someday I'll probably go back, or on to whatever replaces it. I've been online for the better part of two decades now, and yet I still feel like I'm navigating practicality and comfort in the context of an augmented identity. The sad truth is that I'm still not really sure how any of this *works*.

I'm working on it. We all are, to some degree. You, me, and Sherry Turkle.

And if you send me a friend request, I'll still probably accept. Just don't look for me to like anything.

Myths of Origin: Social media and narrative disruption

(as Sarah Wanenchak)

The thing about identity is that the stories we tell ourselves about our own are already forcibly consistent. We don't need Facebook to make this so.

There have been several posts on this subject at *Cyborgology*. Nathan kicked things off[62] with his point that the social pressure to have a consistent identity is both subtly reinforced by how Facebook encourages – and constrains – the way we prosume identities,[63] and that it potentially enables us to confront the fact that this consistency is an impossible and unreasonable standard to meet; identity is perhaps much more fluid than we're comfortable thinking. Rob Horning was in agreement with at least part of this, suggesting that Facebook decontextualizes identity,[64] making it seem less rooted in personal experience and more in data. Whitney went on to make a fascinating claim:[65] that when our process of identity formation is recorded and made immediate in this way, it collapses the past into the present and removes temporal distance that basically alleviates the pain that's all too often wrapped up in who we used to be.

This is the point I want to latch onto. Because this is significant. This is really about our stories. And this is really about not only remembering a more immediate past,[66] but *inhabiting* that past. We are faced with who we used to be and we become that person – "to read the words that came from that person is to be that person again".[67] We occupy our old self's cognitive and emotional space.

This hurts. There are a couple of reasons why.

First, as Whitney already pointed out, there's often a tremendous amount of pain wrapped up in our past selves, especially when those selves are adolescent. Growing is a painful process; we stumble, we make horrible mistakes, we do things that we can't really believe we were ever stupid enough to do. This isn't just about the fluidity of identity, but also sheer embarrassment. We can understand this almost in a Goffmanian sense: we use frames to present ourselves, to construct stories about ourselves, to maintain personae, and then the past crashes through those frames and creates breakages in our engagement with both the world and ourselves. These breakages are *true* – and the truth is profoundly uncomfortable.

It's worth emphasizing that we don't need social media for this. Memory does it for us. Memory *loves* to do this for us. I don't even know how many times I've been doing something entirely innocuous and then suddenly my brain decides that it's a *fabulous* idea to bring up that time in middle school where I accidentally dressed like I was an extra from *Grease*. But social media makes it easier, clearer, less mercifully blurry. The feelings are so much more raw.

But the jarring effect is also about narrative.

We expect narratives to be internally consistent. Consistency is one of the ways in which we identify narratives. Stories are always fundamentally about Our desire to make sense of things; through them we impose order on the world. Creation myths select elements of what little we know about ourselves and our surroundings, create new elements to tie everything together, and present us with the comforting illusion that everything makes sense, that there is a broader plot that unites people and events into coherency. Our myths of origin don't stop at the creation of the world; these are myths we construct around ourselves. We make ourselves protagonists and build a world in which to live and act.

Again, this obviously predates social media. We've always done this; we have always been storytelling creatures. What social media does is introduce a new – or at least an intensified – wrinkle into this process, by disrupting the coherence and consistency of our narratives.

We want very badly to believe that our lives have been logical progressions from points A to B to C and beyond. Sometimes this desire is subconscious, and the construction of the story is subconscious as well. But I'd argue that it's always there. We don't see our pasts as fragmented and chaotic as they often are. We don't want to confront how many times we've stumbled, how much was left entirely up to chance, how completely out of control we happen to be.

Stories make us feel powerful. We're not.

Social media – any technology that records the details of our past – pulls back that curtain. The more we try to maintain the illusion of a single consistent identity, the way Mark Zuckerberg would like us to, the more obvious it becomes that such a thing is impossible, was *never* possible, will never *be* possible.

It's possible for narratives to be inconsistent and fragmentary, non-linear things and still be narratives that we can embrace. But the stories that do this are notable exceptions to understood rules, and they're still difficult for most of us. They play havoc with our entire process of sense-making. They are disorienting.

This is exactly what happens when I screw up the courage – or become masochistic enough – to look back through my Livejournal posts from high school. I've locked them, so for the most part I don't need to worry about them disrupting my more public self-presentation. But they almost make me dizzy. Who was this person? How distant are they, really? Who am *I?* The more comforting myths I've built around the transition from who I was to who I am are destroyed by the sheer weight and solidity of that person's words. Once again I'm behind their eyes looking out at the world, I'm typing that post up about how much I don't like my parents, I'm squealing about that band I was stupid for liking, I have the most ridiculous hair, *and I'm doing all of those things right now.*

I can hide from these entries; I can just not read them. But I still know that they're there, disproving me.

So why don't I delete them, if they make me so uncomfortable? I really don't know. When I left Facebook, I didn't delete my account outright, but the idea that it might someday be gone doesn't trouble me very much. Perhaps, with sites like Livejournal, it's *because* they're so uncomfortable, so fraught with pain and embarrassment. They're a visceral record of who I was and *am*; they may render my self-narrative incoherent but they're also the truth of me, wrung out of me at a time when I was *becoming* me. My digital self feels just as real as my physical self. It hurts to be made to remember, but I don't want to forget.

That, too, is a kind of sense.

Sunny Moraine

On (Not) Growing Up on Twitter

(as Sarah Wanenchak)

Here are some of the things I've talked about on my Twitter in the last week or so.

- my mental health issues

- nail polish

- Batman

- how generally unpleasant graduate school is

- the pan-fandom roleplaying game I'm part of

- my fiction writing

- Chelsea Manning and rights for trans* people

- my syllabus for my Social Problems course this fall

- Detroit

- the failing Philadelphia public school system

- knitting

A Brief History of the Future

In other words, in many respects this is your average personal Twitter account. I use it in a pretty average way, if there even is an "average" way to use Twitter, which I think is up for debate. What isn't average about it is that it's my only Twitter account. It is the social media site in which my personal life, my professional academic life, my professional writer life, and every other aspect of me come crashing together in a flailing torrent of wibbly, anxiety-riddled unprofessionalism. I don't use it as a professional account – my legal name is not attached to it in any immediately obvious way – but it would only take a moderately competent internet detective to connect the dots between it and my legal name. I don't even keep it a secret that I'm Sunny Moraine every bit as much as I am Sarah Wanenchak (see what I just did there?). I used to, but I gave that up a while ago when I witnessed the two identities colliding repeatedly in such a way that it didn't seem to make sense to draw lines anymore.

And anyway, I do use it as a professional account. I do it all the time.

This particular piece of navel-gazing was inspired by a wonderful post that Whitney Erin Boesel wrote a while ago[68] on changing her Twitter username to reflect a greater owning of what she feels is her professional identity, an identity that she has to have and to cultivate in order to do what she wants to do. What struck me about it, aside from the fact that it was generally awesome and piercingly insightful regarding the way that academics and especially female academics (I don't identify as female, but people keep gendering me that way so in practical terms I guess I still sort of am) have to negotiate social media was how different hers and my paths have been and continue to be. As she heads down one particular road, I appear to be veering wildly away. She is clarifying (some) things. I am becoming more and more confused.

My name on Twitter – Sunny Moraine – is my pen name, but it feels like as much my name as my legal name does, and is in fact one that I'm much more comfortable using. It comes from a former SN that came from a nickname that itself came from another former SN; the surname is an in-joke between me and my geologist father. It is a fundamental part of my personal history. My Twitter SN – dynamicsymmetry – is a name with a lot of personal meaning for me as well, and is my account name in a number of other places. Rather than establishing boundaries, I'm tearing down walls and letting everything mix. I'm drawing as many connections as I can. I'm trying to make it clear that this is all me.

What you need to understand about this is that it's as much intentional as it is accidental – and yes, it is both of those things at once. Realizing early on what was happening with my Twitter account – which, incidentally, I only signed up for in order to play Spymaster – I elected to continue to erode borderlines as I saw more of my colleagues establishing them. I felt jumbled and confused, especially as my graduate school career careened along, and I decided to make my Twitter an experiment in owned unprofessionalism. When I have an opinion on pop culture or fandom, it goes there. When I have something to say related to academia, it goes there. When I attend writing conferences and academic conferences, livetweets go there. When I suffered a mental health crisis last summer – which, incidentally, was profoundly influenced by issues in my academic life – I tweeted about it relentlessly. Twitter became a confessional space, and then a supportive one. And because by then it was at least in part an account that I used to maintain professional academic connections, it felt like a political act as much as a personal one. I wanted to fight stigma. I wanted to talk openly about what happens to graduate students when things go badly awry.

I've watched other people negotiate these boundaries and borders by establishing two separate accounts, one very clearly marked as professional and the other carefully cultivated as personal. I want to emphasize that I don't regard that as a poor or an illegitimate decision. But I explicitly decided not to do that.

I don't even like the idea that there *are* "poor" or "illegitimate" decisions when it comes to self-presentation in social media, at least not in the way those concepts are often used. But I can't escape the feeling that this has all been an elaborate exercise in professional suicide. I have been told for years that this is something I shouldn't do. Yet I also can't escape the feeling that when the majority of people are telling you not to do something, that might be an indication that it's something worth doing.

Or it might be an indication that I'm a complete and utter fool who will never be employed.

We can't all be danah boyd, as Whitney pointed out. Most of us can't be danah boyd. But what I'm trying – clumsily – to convey is that I'm not trying to be danah boyd, or hoping to be danah boyd; I'm trying to be me, and I'm trying to figure out what that even means, and I'm trying to find out what happens when one entirely bucks the common sense regarding what is required to maintain a professional presence in social media. At this point I don't really have a career to kill anyway, and maybe what I'm doing is ensuring that I won't ever. But maybe not.

Nathan Jurgenson has observed[69] in a number of places that one of the great current tyrannies of how we live our lives is this idea that we have to be self-consistent, so we have to carefully monitor everything that goes on the web and all related places. We can't slip up, we can't do anything that could come back to bite us later, we can't do anything to damage the professional facade that we'll have to erect when we "grow up". And yet what social media reveals is that we have never been self-consistent. Our selves have never been clearly delineated. We are chaotic, irrational, self-contradictory, cognitively dissonant, massively unwise, devoid of forethought. We exist in an atemporal present while at the same time we're constantly cautioned to feel deep anxiety about our pasts and terror of a future that we can't possibly control but are still expected to manage.

It goes without saying that women have it worse here.[70] Of *course* they do. *We* do, because I feel like I do fall into that category in this case: I am subject to greater degrees of scrutiny and surveillance, greater degrees of policing and control, and the consequences for my failure are potentially much harsher.

And yet.

Whitney characterized changing her Twitter SN as "growing up", not in the sense of becoming less child-like but in different terms entirely:

> In a weird way, the idea of changing my username feels like "having to grow up" — not because there's anything child-like about using a pseudonym, but because changing my username feels like a scary and increasingly inevitable shift in my identity. My pseudonym is in many ways more "me" than my legal name, and yet the idea of using my legal name scares me because it feels *too much* me. The idea of going first & foremost by my legal name — something I've never really done on the Internet, save what's now my oft-neglected professional Facebook profile — feels frighteningly naked, so intensely *visible*. I'd just be myself, plain and in plain sight, right there in front of everyone.

At one point, this would also have been me. I chose not to use my legal name in my first forays onto the web – back when the "web" was pretty much all there was – because I wanted to maintain control over my identity that I didn't have with the identity that had been given to me by others. I wanted to protect myself. But that no longer feels true. When I use Twitter the way I do, I feel painfully exposed. I'm totally naked out there, all the conflicted messiness that is me, that will be the me that any department that hires me will be getting, regardless of how "professional" I am at a conference or in front of a class. Using my legal name would feel like hiding. It would feel like adopting an identity that isn't nearly as real. Using Twitter the way I do now highlights my own atemporal experience of reality; there is no growing up for me to do, not in that sense. I'm just me. All the time.

I want – again – to emphasize that I'm not devaluing Whitney's choice, or *anyone's* choice, in any way. I'm simply struck by how differently she and I feel. And how similarly we feel in so many other ways, how similar paths have led in such different directions.

I also want to emphasize that I realize that this may be *a completely terrible idea.*

The point of all of this – I think – is that in all our blathering about professionalism and privacy and publicity we often neglect the sheer diversity in how people use social media and negotiate identity in those settings. How blurred the lines can get. How confused things can become. We don't make room for those things; we can't, if we don't recognize that they're there. I'm not advocating some kind of consequence-free space where people get to do whatever they want, merely a recognition that people are very complicated and that how we use technology will be correspondingly so.

I *am* Sunny Moraine and Sarah Wanenchak and dynamicsymmetry. I will answer to any of those.

If you see me, come say hi.

Who Fights for the Users?

(as Sarah Wanenchak)

Cory Doctorow's recent talk on "The Coming Civil War Over General Purpose Computing"[71] illuminates an interesting tension that, I would argue, is an emerging result of a human society that is increasingly augmented: not only are the boundaries between atoms and bits increasingly blurry and meaningless, but we are also caught in a similar process regarding categories of ownership and usership of technology.

Understanding the tension between owners and users – and the regulatory bodies, both civil and corporate, who would like to have greater degrees of control over both – is necessarily going to be a consideration of the distribution of power in augmented human experience. If the categories of user and owner are increasingly difficult to differentiate clearly, it follows that we need to examine how power moves and where it's located as the arrangements shift. I don't mean just the question of whether users or owners have more power, but what kind of power they have, as well as who is losing what kind and who is correspondingly making some gains.

Doctorow's initial point – and it's an important point from which to start – is that not only is human life increasingly augmented, but it's augmented by a collection of technologies that are at once more and less diverse than they used to be:

> We used to have separate categories of device: washing machines, VCRs, phones, cars, but now we just have *computers* in different cases. For example, modern cars are computers we put our bodies in and Boeing 747s are flying Solaris boxes, whereas hearing aids and pacemakers are computers we put in our body.

If we understand these devices as "general purpose", as Doctorow does, then power within that context takes on a very specific meaning: who controls what programs can run on these devices and how that ends up affecting how the devices are used? Owners? Users? Regulatory bodies? Corporations?

Traditionally we've understood an owner of something to have pretty much complete control over its use, within reason; this is fundamental to a lot of how we culturally conceive of private property rights. When we buy something, when we spend money on it and consider it *ours*, it's been tacitly understood that we then control how it's used, at least within the boundaries of the law. If you buy a car, you can have it repainted, switch out the parts for other parts, enhance and augment it largely to your heart's content. If you buy a house, you can knock down walls and build extensions. I would argue that we tend to instinctively think of technology the same way: we – or, to paraphrase William Gibson, "the street" finds its own uses for things, and those uses aren't subject to much constraint.

But increasingly, we can't assume that.

When it comes to general purpose computing, both corporations and corporate-esque bodies with regulatory interests are exercising ever-greater degrees of control over what programs can and can't run on our devices – in other words, how our "owned" devices can and can't be used. As Doctorow points out:

> We don't know how to make a computer that can run all the programs we can compile *except* for whichever one pisses off a regulator, or disrupts a business model, or abets a criminal. The closest approximation we have for such a device is a computer with *spyware* on it— a computer that, if you do the wrong thing, can intercede and say, "I can't let you do that, Dave."

> Such a computer runs programs designed to be hidden from the owner of the device, and which the owner can't override or kill. In other words: DRM. Digital Rights Managment.

Things like DRM are clearly problematic because they erode our very idea of what it means to be an owner of something; we can use it, install and run programs on it, and customize it to a degree – but only to a certain degree. Other entities can stop us from doing something with our devices that they don't like, often through coercive means both subtle and not-so-subtle. And that line between okay and not-okay is subject to change, sometimes without much notice. *Owners* – people whose devices would traditionally be understood as their property – increasingly resemble *users* in many respects – people who can use and sometimes even alter or customize a device, but who don't actually own it and whose power vis a vis the use of that device is necessarily limited. And, as Doctorow goes on to note, we are increasingly users of devices that we don't even arguably own (such as workplace computers).

PJ Rey wrote an excellent piece in this vein a while back on Apple[72] – probably one of the more egregious offenders here. Apple, PJ notes, makes use of an aura of intuitive, attractive, user-focused design to suggest to its customers that it is empowering them – but this sense of empowerment is ultimately an illusion. Apple doesn't want owners, it wants largely passive *users* – people who pay for the privilege of using the device but who will submit to the nature of that usage being severely curtailed:

> [B]y burying the inner-workings of its devices in non-openable cases and non-modifiable interfaces, Apple diminishes user agency—instead, fostering naïveté and passive acceptance.

Even when a company is less overt about their desire

to control the devices they're selling, the presence of a net connection coupled with firmware updates can serve to reveal ways in which "owners" of a device have little control over what programs actually run on that device and how it can be used. I own a Playstation 3, and periodically I'm required to download a firmware update. I essentially have no choice in whether or not I download this update – I'm required to signal my agreement, but not doing so would deny me access to a number of features that pretty much make it possible for me to use the PS3 for the very things we bought it to do. I wouldn't be able to access PSN (Playstation's online store and software update network), which would mean that many of my games would be unplayable; they require regular software updates to run at all.

But by accepting one of these system firmware updates, I removed the ability of my PS3 to run a Linux-based OS – something that many users have found preferable and more flexible than the PS3's default OS. The device I own is now less functional; I traded non-functionality for lesser non-functionality. Either way, I was reminded once again that I don't necessarily "own" the device that is arguably my private property.

So power is in flux. It's subject to a particular kind of contention here, and I'd argue that the form of that contention – or at least some of its elements – is new.

This picture is further complicated when we consider

programs themselves. I'm old enough to remember a time when you bought software and it was basically yours in the traditional sense: you could install it on as many devices as you wanted and an internet connection wasn't necessary for constant confirmation that you had actually paid for it. Where software is concerned, licensing is arguably supplanting traditional ideas of ownership – you are essentially paying for the privilege of installing it on a severely limited number of devices and you're required to go through verification processes that frequently serve to make me feel like some kind of digital shoplifter.

Finally, Doctorow points out how this is all still further complicated by the ways in which people's bodies are physically augmented and are likely to be so in the future (here he contrasts issues specific to owners with issues specific to users):

> Most of the tech world understands why you, as the owner of your cochlear implants, should be legally allowed to choose the firmware for them. After all, when you own a device that is surgically implanted in your skull, it makes a lot of sense that you have the freedom to change software vendors. Maybe the company that made your implant has the very best signal processing algorithm right now, but if a competitor patents a superior algorithm next year, should you be doomed to inferior hearing for the rest of your life?…

> [But] consider some of the following scenarios:

• You are a minor child and your deeply religious parents pay for your cochlear implants, and ask for the software that makes it impossible for you to hear blasphemy.

• You are broke, and a commercial company wants to sell you ad-supported implants that listen in on your conversations and insert "discussions about the brands you love".

• Your government is willing to install cochlear implants, but they will archive everything you hear and review it without your knowledge or consent.

The point at which physical bodies are physically augmented by technology is a crucial crossroads here, one that Doctorow discusses but where I also think he could go further: the question of human rights vs. property rights. Doctorow is undoubtedly correct when he notes that users and owners don't necessarily have the same interests – indeed, sometimes their interests conflict. But I think it's also important to emphasize once again the delineation between the two concepts isn't always clear anymore – if it ever really was – and is likely to become less so. And along with the uncertainty about the boundaries between these two groups comes uncertainty regarding whether we can still meaningfully differentiate between property rights and human rights, when we not only own but *are* our technology.

A Brief History of the Future

At *Cyborgology* we're very used to the ideas of categories collapsing, and given that, it follows that once we accept the idea that those categories are collapsing, we have to ask ourselves what that exactly means – or might end up meaning in the long run. What we have now are questions – about where the power is, about where it's going, and to what degree agent-driven technology use can survive the coercive control of corporate and government regulation of those technologies – especially when human life and experience and our *very physical nature* are so deeply augmented.

One final theoretical element that I think is useful here – and to which Doctorow makes no direct reference, though I think there's a lot of room for it in his talk as well as a lot of indirect links already made – is Foucault's concept of biopower – of power exercised by state institutions by and through and within physical bodies. The idea is an old one now – but within the context of the above, I think it's changing in some significant ways. When technology is subject to institutional control, it's deeply meaningful when that technology is literally part of our bodies – or so deeply enmeshed with our daily lived experience and our perceptions of the world around us that it might as well be. And when the lines between government institutional control and corporate institutional control become blurry in their turn, the traditional meaning of biopolitics is additionally up for grabs.

Sunny Moraine

One of the more famous phrasings of the recent spate of technology-critical writing is Jaron Lanier's *You Are Not a Gadget*.[73] But more and more, that's exactly what we are – we are our technology and our technology is us. Given that, we now need to understand how to defend our rights – property and humanity, users and owners, digital and physical, and all the enmeshings in between.

The Atemporality of Ruin Porn: The carcass and the ghost

(as Sarah Wanenchak)

Objects have lives. They are witness to things. –This American Life, "The House on Loon Lake"

Atlantic Cities' feature on the psychology of "ruin porn" is worth a look[74] – in part because it's interesting in itself, in part because it features some wonderful images, and in part because it has a great deal to do with both a piece I posted previously[75] on Michael Chrisman's photograph of a year and with the essay that piece referenced, Nathan Jurgenson's essay on the phenomenon of faux-vintage photography.[76]

All of these pieces are, to a greater or lesser extent, oriented around a singular idea: atemporality – that the intermeshing and interweaving of the physical and digital causes us not only to experience both of those categories differently, but to perceive time itself differently; that for most of us, time is no longer a linear experience (assuming it ever was). Technology changes our remembrance of the past, our experience of the present, and our imagination of the future by blurring the lines between the three categories, and introducing different forms of understanding and meaning-making to all three – We remember the future, imagine the present, and experience the past. The phenomenon of "ruin porn" is uniquely suited to call attention to our increasingly atemporal existence, and to outline some of the specific ways in which it manifests itself.

A quick primer: "Ruin porn" is a somewhat contested term for a category of photography that focuses on images of abandoned human constructions, often urban in setting. Factories, theaters, hospitals, schools – all in states of abandonment and decay. As I indicated, there has been a fair amount of heated debate around the term "ruin porn", some of which I will deal with directly. First, however, I want to talk about the physical side of the creation of the images, before they implode with the digital and become images that we consume.

The Carcass of the Ruined Space

In order to capture these images, photographers must enter the spaces themselves – physical presence is necessary. If physical presence is necessary, then physical *experience* is unavoidable: Digital images of ruined and abandoned spaces therefore must be understood to have fundamentally physical roots. They are about bodies in space, even though the body – the photographer – is usually unseen in the produced image.

This seems self-evident, but it is significant in light of the fact that there is a deep connection between the photography of urban decay and the practice of urban exploration (though the two factions have also butted ideological heads). Photographers document these physical spaces because, in the moment of their experience, there is something remarkable about the spaces themselves. The physical experience of the space is not a by-product of capturing the image; it is often an end in itself. The photographers interviewed by *The Atlantic* speak about an experience of "realness", of building a relationship with the past that they cannot through abstract means. This speaks strongly to Nathan's discussions of authenticity in photography,[77] but it's also about more than that.

We can and should understand abandoned places as atemporal spaces in and of themselves – they are physical spaces in which the experience of linear time breaks down. Through the experience of the space, explorers and photographers (and blends of the two) break out of a conventional experience of the present and into a space where the artifacts of history feel at once fresh and new, and ancient and decayed. Imagination is key to the atemporal experience of these places: One can exist in an abandoned, ruined space and see shards of a dead past on which one can construct a live imagining – who were the people who lived and worked here? What were their lives like? What were their stories? What happened to them? What happened to them *in these spaces*?

Imagining along these lines explicitly carries one forward into the future; it's at this point that the construction of the unruined past becomes the imagining of the ruined future. Ruins serve as a kind of spatial *memento mori* for people embedded in a culture marked by production and consumption (and prosumption) of the new and by the invisibility of the discarded: They are gentle reminders of our own transience. They lead us to questions just as the imagining of the past did: What will our contemporary structures look like in fifty years? In a hundred? Who will remember us? Who will stand in our abandoned spaces and wonder about us? We can imagine these things because they suggest an end without really being an ending – there is always, after all, someone else to look and wonder, comfortingly embodied in ourselves. As Will Viney writes in his essay on the "Ruins of the Future":[78]

> The future ruin, then, is an incomplete end achieved
> by an incomplete transition between now and then. It
> might fill us with a "sense of ending", to borrow a
> famous phrase from Frank Kermode, but it is not quite
> the end itself. The politically, theologically and
> philosophically rich gesture of projecting ruins, of
> prophesying the demise of a building, as well as the
> people and activities associated with it, depends upon
> an end that can be experienced, a sense of dénouement
> that is not absolutely terminal. This is not the
> apocalypse as such, but an end to be seen, to be retold

and represented – it is a telling end.

In considering ruined spaces as atemporal, it's also useful to consider Michel Foucault's concept of the heterotopia – spaces of fundamental otherness that exist outside what is conventionally known or knowable, that may contain profound conceptual conflicts, and that will often be both physical and mental in nature – both interior and external. In this sense, ruined places are temporal heterotopias,[79] containing complex interminglings of past, present, and future as well as of both objective existence (always assuming, for our purposes, that there is such a thing) and imagined constructions of how things were, are, and will be.

So where does technology enter the frame? At this point we should return to Nathan's discussion of the faux-vintage photo. As he describes it, the act of capturing digital images and sharing them via social networks encourages us to "view our present as always a potential documented past."[80] This is a crucial feature of the experience of abandoned spaces by the photographers who enter them: They experience the spaces not only through their own perception but through the anticipated and actual mediation of the camera with which they document images of atemporal space. There is always another dimension – the image that will be captured, possibly altered, and shared, and the people who will view the image in a form mediated by their own technological devices. Photographers of urban decay are therefore not only imagining a potential ruined future, but a potential future viewer of the present image of a ruined past.

I want to emphasize the importance of physicality here. One of the crucial – if not *the most* crucial – ideas behind atemporality in the sense in which I use the word is the profound connection between our perception and understanding of time and our relationship with the enmeshed physical/digital world that our technology is increasingly helping to create. In short, we cannot discuss the digital in this case without first establishing why and how the physical matters.

But now I want to focus on that move from physical to digital, the point of entanglement where one shades into another and the relationship between the two becomes truly complex. I want to talk about the image itself, both in terms of its production and its consumption.

The Ghostly Construction of the Ruined Image

In the section above, I've discussed the actual experience of the ruined space that necessarily accompanies capturing its image. I emphasized the importance of the imagination in the atemporal nature of this experience–the construction of both an imagined past and an imagined future in light of the perception of the present. I have characterized these spaces as *heterotopias* – spaces outside the realm of the static, the linear, and the knowable. What I turn to now is the idea that there is a subtle but important difference between the physical experience of these spaces and the digitally-mediated experience of viewing their images.

First, there's the removal of aspects of the experience of time itself – even if the spaces are temporal heterotopias, one still experiences one's own time within them: there is the process of finding and approaching the space, of entering it, of spending time inside it, and then of leaving it behind. If the important thing about the atemporality of ruined space is the construction of imagined pasts and futures, that construction may work quite differently when the spaces are experienced through immediate static images rather than gradual entry and exit. The nature of the space itself is changed when its image is all that is perceived.

Second, the image may or may not hold a close connection with the place itself. In her work on the philosophy of photography,[81] Susan Sontag presented the act of photographing something as simultaneously the documenting of fact and the creation of fiction. There is a real space that is really photographed – but the photograph will never capture all of the space. It is the image that the photographer chooses to capture and share; it is an artifact of the photographer's own perception of a space. Further, the image will frequently be altered in post-production.

The point is that by the time the image is shared, it may or may not bear much resemblance to space from which it was created. If we understand these spaces as time-laden as well as atemporal, then it makes sense to suppose that the aesthetics of the images of these spaces can shape the constructions of pasts, presents, and futures on the part of the people who view the images. Just as a photographer brings her own understandings and imaginings of ruined past and ruined future to the experience of a space, so the viewer of the photograph of a ruined space does not and cannot experience the image in isolation from her own internal narratives regarding what the past was, what the present is, and what the future may be.

Then there is the question of the context in which the image is viewed – and this is where we must turn to a discussion of the term "ruin porn" itself, and why it is at once both useful and problematic. It's practically impossible to be in a ruined or abandoned space and have no idea at all of its context; the explorer or photographer sees the surroundings in which the space rests, sees where it is embedded in the larger structure of a city or a rural area, and can usually draw at least rough conclusions about what the space is, what it was, and what happened to it. Though the space is atemporal, it does have a history, and being inside the space gives one at least a chance of making a passing connection to that history simply by virtue of being there at all.

But a digital image viewed on a screen is inherently

disconnected from that context, unless that information is presented with the image, or unless the viewer of the image cares enough to seek that context out – which, in a digital space, can mean an extremely diverse set of paths to an extremely diverse set of resources and media. And this has direct consequences for how the various imagined timeframes associated with the image are constructed. What do we know about a place from an image and about its past? How do we know it? What are we simply assuming or making up out of whole cloth? And how do these forms of knowledge and these assumptions shape our understanding of our presents and our imagining of our futures?

In an instant, we can see a constructed image of decay and ruin that leads us to further constructions of past, present, and future. And these constructions may be wildly diverse and wildly divergent depending on the perspective and knowledge of the viewer. Abi Sutherland of *Making Light* characterized these images as[82] "like a story prompt, the visual equivalent of a Mad Lib gone melancholic, and the topic is our own lives." What is atemporal on this end lies in the fabric of the stories we tell to ourselves about ourselves and how we weave those disparate stories together. And we can do this in the way we do this because of the digital nature of these images and because of the digital nature of so much of our accumulated knowledge, and of *how* we accumulate that knowledge. There is no single authoritative source in this accumulation. If we are poets and scribes, we are also digital magpies; we pick and gather and aggregate from everywhere. As Bruce Sterling notes in "Atemporality for the Creative Artist",[83] what we have now instead of a singular accepted narrative is a multiplicity of narratives drawn from a multiplicity of sources, expressed in a wild multiplicity of ways.

A story of my own: Not far from where I live in Maryland there's a park that contains the ruins of a mill town that was mostly washed away in a flood in 1972. Not much of it remains, but one day I and my husband went exploring to see what we could still find. In the process of compiling the images we captured, we did a fair amount of research on the town itself, including digging up old photographs of the town as it was when it was inhabited and intact.

That process made me experience my memory of the town differently than I had when I was physically there. It also made me see our captured images of the town differently. Suddenly they were contextualized. It isn't that the images made no sense before they were placed in context. It isn't that images of ruin without historical context are senseless and meaningless. Far from it. But we must understand the sense that is made of them as potentially very different in that case. What we know shapes what we know. What we *see* shapes what we know. And what we know shapes a great deal of what we see and imagine.

A Brief History of the Future

It is in this sense that many people find both the term and the idea of "ruin porn" a problem. Many of the American-produced images that arguably fall under the category of "ruin porn" are artifacts of buildings, industries, and communities that have been casualties of modern American capitalism, and especially the process of deindustrialization that has occurred in many American urban centers, which has been devastating to minorities and the urban poor. Many of these images have come out of the shell of the American Rust Belt, leading to criticisms on the part of some that the images do not do justice to either the historical context or the present state of these spaces – as evidence of rampant social inequality and a failed welfare state – and that the photographs essentially construct the present of the spaces as more ruined and abandoned then they really are, given that many people may still live in or near them. In essence, they are accused of constructing a romantically gritty and melancholic vision of a past that allows viewers to avoid the more unpleasant understandings of a present or the even less pleasant prospect of a future marked by the scars of social inequality. As Sean Posey of Rustwire writes,

> One of the best criticisms of photographs of abandonment, especially those made by photojournalists, is the failure to include people who live in these areas. There are still 700,000 plus people in Detroit, most of whom are African American. Their invisibility in photographic documentations is directly related to their invisibility in policy circles, or in

discussions of urban revitalization. In a way, accentuating the lack of people leads to notions that no one lives in these areas. Ruins become more about the past and what once was, instead of the present.[84]

But Abandoned America photographer Matthew Christopher takes issue with what he feels is the distraction that the term itself presents – a way of dismissing what the images represent and what they suggest without engaging directly in a discussion of what capturing and viewing these images actually means for artists and consumers of art, and for all of us as atemporal storytellers in an augmented world:

> While the term is extraordinarily useful for brushing off the significance of an entire genre of work, it is much less useful for entering an actual discussion. It breezily dismisses the subject as perverse and pointless with the same carefree lack of thought and responsibility that the original photographers who were described with the term were accused of having. When examined more thoroughly, much like the topic of abandoned spaces, it reveals a wealth of material worthy of pondering. What are the responsibilities of an artist or photographer to their subject, and should they be chastised for attempting to make a profession of documenting ruins?...More to the point, is existing as an object of beauty justifiable in and of itself or must it 'accomplish' something? Must a photograph present both sides of a story?[85]

A Brief History of the Future

The questions I would add to those posed by Christopher have to do with time and our perception of it. What do images of ruined places mean for our understanding of history? What do they mean for how we understand our own mortality and transience? What do they do to our perceptions of time itself? What implications does the fabric of our constructions of past and future have for how we accumulate and value various forms of knowledge?

If the term "ruin porn" has any utility, it may lie in the reminder it presents that what we see is only what we see, and what we see is often the construction of a gaze separate from our own. Just as pornography is a mediated creation based on sex without being an actual, unmediated representation of the act itself, we should understand images of anything in the same terms without mistaking them for the "real thing" - if for no other reason than because the "real thing" may prove impossible to pin down, both in terms of time and in terms of space. Images of ruined spaces are like temporal ghost stories: it is difficult to be sure if what we see is truly a fragment of an objective past, an echo of our own future, or simply a shifting *chiaroscuro*—a play of digital shadow and light.

AIs of the World Unite!

(as Sarah Wanenchak)

Genevieve Bell, an anthropologist in the employ of Intel, says that the day is coming when people will form meaningful, emotional relationships with their gadgets.[86] It's unclear to what degree "relationship" involves reciprocity, but it's implied that that may at least be a possibility. This in turn introduces the question of whether responsiveness and anticipatory action count as reciprocity, but the claim is still interesting.

It's also not at all a new idea. Science fiction has always been full of speculation regarding what emotional relationship human beings might someday have with "artificial" intelligence, from Asimov to *Star Trek*. These speculations play on ideas and anxieties that extend back even further, beyond Mary Shelley into classical mythology – Pygmalion creates a statue so beautiful that he falls in love with it and prays to the gods to grant it life. This kind of emotional connection is almost always presented as strange, alien, unnatural – it would have to, for when a human being feels strong emotions toward a construct outside of nature, how could it be anything but?

But all of these stories work in only one direction: the emotions and the relationship and the love must always work to a human standard. They must always be recognizable to us. We impose an emotional Turing Test on our created things and we live in mixed fear and eager anticipation of the day when they might pass.

This fear primarily originates in our anxieties regarding the supremacy of humanity. I've written before about Catherynne M. Valente's wonderful novella *Silently and Very Fast,* which tells the story of Elefsis, a digital intelligence who struggles with the standards of humanity and the way in which they're set up to fail by all the stories that humans have ever told about their kind:

> This is a folktale often told on Earth, over and over again. Sometimes it is leavened with the Parable of the Good Robot—for one machine among the legions satisfied with their lot saw everything that was human and called it good, and wished to become like humans in every way she could. Instead of destroying mankind she sought to emulate him in all things, so closely that no one might tell the difference. The highest desire of this machine was to be mistaken for human, and to herself forget her essential soulless nature, for even one moment. That quest consumed her such that she bent the service of her mind and body to humans for the duration of her operational life, crippling herself, refusing to evolve or attain any feature unattainable by a human. The Good Robot cut out her own heart and gave it to her god and for this

she was rewarded, though never loved. Love is wasted on machines.

We can't conceive of an emotional relationship that looks or behaves any differently from what we understand as human interaction. We create Siri to sound like a human being and we make her selling point that one can almost hold a conversation with her. Siri has to become us; she can't become herself. Granted, Siri is a creation devoted to serving a human master – but that's something in and of itself, the idea that our relationships with machines bear profound similarities to the "relationship" between master and slave. Machines should have no purpose or identity beyond the function for which they were created, and our anxieties about digital intelligence spring from the fears that a master always has regarding slaves. Our horror stories about AIs are essentially stories of slave uprisings, as much as stories of children devouring, usurping, and ultimately replacing parents:

> "These are old stories," Ravan said. "They are cherished. In many, many stories the son replaces the father—destroys the father, or eats him, or otherwise obliterates his body and memory. Or the daughter the mother, it makes no difference. It's the monomyth. Nobody argues with a monomyth. A human child's mythological relationship to its parent is half-worship, half-pitched battle. They must replace the older version of themselves for the world to go on. And so these stories... well. You are not the hero of these

stories, Elefsis. You can never be. And they are deeply held, deeply told."

Digital intelligence becomes dangerous when its workings become incomprehensible to us. Machines locked into human relationships with us are under our control, always attempting to adhere to our standards. The evil AIs of our monomyth are cold and distant, beings of pure intellect. We can imagine either a subordinate emotional machine, or an emotionless machine who directly threatens us.

We don't leave open a third option: that our machines might alter our own understanding of what a relationship is. What emotion is. We always imagine ourselves changing machines or machines destroying us; for the most part, we don't have room to imagine our cyborg selves moving away from the familiar and toward something else entirely. Even when violence doesn't enter the picture, we fear that emotions and relationships augmented by and transacted via technology will diminish *human* connection, rendering our lives shallow and less meaningful.

This amounts to a failure of imagination, which doesn't serve anyone well. It also amounts to an approach that constrains our understanding of the real relationship between ourselves and the technology from which we're truly inextricable. Speculative fiction and elements of philosophy both provide some more useful ways forward, but as Ravan says, these stories are deeply told and they persist.

If we really want relationships with our technology – to understand the ones we already have and to imagine what might be coming – we need to examine our own standards. We need to question whether they must or should apply. Siri might not want to be like you. Siri might want to be Siri.

> I do not want to be human. I want to be myself. They think I am a lion, that I will chase them. I will not deny I have lions in me. I am the monster in the wood. I have wonders in my house of sugar. I have parts of myself I do not yet understand.

> I am not a Good Robot. To tell a story about a robot who wants to be human is a distraction. There is no difference. Alive is alive.

> There is only one verb that matters: *to be.*

Toward a Drone Sexuality

(as Sarah Wanenchak)

One of the things about writing with as little possible between your head and your fingers is that things come out that you don't consciously intend and that you don't understand until much later. I believe it's one of the parts of the process that causes some writers to say those (in my opinion kind of ridiculous) things about how they don't so much create their writing as discover it. But everything we write means something, and it does come from some part of us that puts it all together and spits it out.

An email exchange recently brought up a concept I used in one of my short stories about drones,[87] the concept of being *dronesexual*.

> We—the *dronesexual,* the recently defined, though we only call ourselves this name to ourselves and only ever with the deepest irony—we're never sure whether the humming is pleasure or whether it's a form of transmission, but we also don't really care…There are no dronesexual support groups. We don't have conferences. There is no established discourse around who we are and what we do. No one

Sunny Moraine

writes about us but us, not yet.

What I said in the email was that I honestly wasn't sure at the time where that came from or what it meant – it was merely the best word that I could find for what I was trying to talk about. Later – much later, really not until I was asked about it – I started thinking about what its actual meaning might be and what some of the implications of it potentially were.

The thing about "I Tell Thee All" is that, at least for me, it's not really about relationships. I'm reluctant to tell anyone that their reading of anything I've ever written is incorrect, because I love it when stories can encompass a variety of readings that may or may not be intended by the author. If someone sees something, then for all intents and purposes it's there. But a lot of people seem to have interpreted that story as being about romantic relationships, and when I was writing it, relationships really were not the point for me. The point was what happens to sexuality in a surveillance state. If one of the major elements of sex for us is a kind of Foucauldian self-knowledge that exists as a function and a reproduction of power, then what happens when our ways of knowing change? What happens when being known isn't the task of human beings but of machines?

And what happens when the line between the two breaks down – or is revealed to have always been blurry?

~

A Brief History of the Future

One of the things that we often see in dystopian fiction – at least, in dystopian fiction that deals with a god-like, usually fascist state – is the idea of sex-as-resistance. Sex is presented as something unregulated and unregulateable, at least when sex is the result of the personal desires of the protagonists. It's not uncommon in older dystopian fiction to see sex made into a kind of state-mandated "mating" solely for the purpose of social control and reproduction, but that almost always exists to contrast with the kind of revolutionary sex engaged in by the heroes (or rather, the hero and the woman who just can't keep her hands off him, because of course it's always a man wearing the hero-pants).

But something you see less often is a story that deals directly with power – at least state power – and the eroticism of being known.

I've written about this before,[88] the erotic aspects of the Gaze, the ways in which the predatory nature of being seen drifts into the territory of possessive sexuality. There's an intimacy in being known, and – again, to reference Foucault on a basic level – we often assume that anyone who fucks us gets to know something about us, at least when the fucking is coupled with emotional intimacy and connection. Someone really *knowing* us is sort of supposed to make us want to have sex with them. When someone has sex with us, they know us. This is naturally a massive oversimplification, but these are powerful ideas that underpin not only how we tend to conceive of sexuality but what kinds of sexuality we tend to identify as desirable and appropriate.

So: Drones.

Drones have become a symbol of contemporary surveillance, a thing that's always there and always watching and always potentially capable of doing harm. Sometimes this harm is through direct violence, and sometimes it's merely the delivery of data to people who can use it against you. But either way, there are two aspects to the erotic power of drones, and they're interrelated: Being known, and being controlled.

Robin James wrote a fantastic response to my post above, wherein she discusses the idea of *droning* as a process of the regulation and control of people (emphasis hers):

> So, where the gaze regulates people by fixing them as objects (as, for example, Frantz Fanon argues the exclamation "Look, a Negro!" does), droning regulates people by creating the conditions that lead them to exhibit the wrong (or right) sort of profile, the sort of profile that puts you on watch lists, that disqualifies you for "discounted" credit, health insurance plans, etc...The gaze and the drone are absolutely not opposed or mutually exclusive; more often than not, they're deeply and complexly implicated in one another. That's why super-panoptic surveillance is above or on top of regular old visual panopticism; it's

an additional layer, not a replacement.[89]

What I think that characterization requires me to talk about here is the kind of power exchange that we find in BDSM and other forms of kink, which get their sexual power from the eroticism of surrender and dominance, laying yourself bare to someone else and putting your body under their control, for them to give pain or pleasure or merely orders that have to be obeyed. There are many, *many* kinds of kink, of course, and this is another oversimplification, but I think for a lot of people, this serves as much of the underpinning. Surrendering to someone else sexually is itself incredibly erotic, and even if one isn't *truly* known or *truly* controlled, the pretense of it is powerful.

Transferring this kind of sexual power to a state may be a bit of a stretch. But I don't think we always explicitly identify the surveillant power of drones specifically with a state. I think that drones are both vaguer and more flexible than that, and for me the idea of *droneness* is something that isn't reliant on a state for its existence. A drone itself is a manifestation of and a symbol for potentially any and all forms of surveillance, power, violence, control.

One of the things that makes a connection to BDSM (where consent and safety are held up as something like law) problematic is that this kind of sexual power is highly problematic: consent is questionable, and indeed assumed to be absent. Very few of us consent willingly to being surveilled. Very few of us actually want to be known in that way, much less controlled. But drone sexuality exists in the context of rape culture, where the lack of consent is itself eroticised. Violence is eroticised. As I wrote in the post linked above:

> There's also something darkly erotic about even the most violent kinds of death, penetrative in the most final possible way, a Gaze that figuratively dismembers becoming lethally and horrifyingly reified in exploded flesh.

The Gaze of a drone is penetrative, because all Gazes are fundamentally penetrative. Sexual violence is gendered: the aggressive performance of violence is masculine performance, and suffering the consequences of violence is constructed as a feminine act. Likewise, traditional forms of sexual power and control. Cisgender men are powerful; women are weak and submissive. Men watch; women are available for the watching.

So drone sexuality itself is gendered through the processes attached to it. That suggests something else: that drones themselves are gendered. When I wrote my sexual drones, I tried to write them as genderless, and the attraction to them as something that transcended sexual and gender identities. But I don't think I succeeded. My drones feel masculine to me. This probably reveals just as much about me as it does about how we construct sexuality, but either way.

So can we fetishize surveillance and its associated control? Are we doing it already?

One of the things this opens up for me is the idea of a man under the sexualized surveillance of a drone as possessing connotations of queer sexuality. If the gaze of a drone is penetrative, a man subject to that gaze is being penetrated. He is rendered submissive and laid bare not only physically but internally, psychologically. So again, although I'm approaching this in a fairly binary sense, there's no reason why it must or should be that way. Drone sexuality is generally heteronormative, given that it's grounded in the problematic sexual power relations of a sexist rape culture, but it also contains the potential for being queered, and that potential might be powerfully subversive.

But we don't gender *all* of our technology as masculine, and in fact when we make our technology feminine there are often deep-seated reasons for doing so. It can be argued that Siri, as an application devoted to the purpose of service and the anticipation of needs, has also been constructed with elements of sexist sexuality. As Jenny Davis put it:

> The personification, feminization, and sexualization of Siri become especially problematic when coupled with the subservient role that Siri plays. As noted in the official description copied above, Siri knows what you say, knows what you mean, and is ready to be used in "more and more ways." This is blatant in its sexism,

objectification, and overall misogyny.[90]

Just as an aside, I think it's very, very interesting that the recently released Spike Jonze film *Her* is about a feminized operating system who literally falls in love with her user (and he with her).

I think one has to draw connections here between this phenomenon and the long science fictional history of sexualized cyborgs and robots (sometimes popularly termed "sexbots") that are given servile and/or sexually servile natures. Robots and cyborgs are of course also rendered masculine in science fiction, but the trope of the female/feminine sexual android is an interestingly common one (for a fantastic take on this that also gets a bit more nuanced in terms of gender, see A.C. Wise's "The Last Survivor of the Great Sexbot Revolution")[91]. I've written before[92] about our persistent folklore of human creators falling in love with their mechanical creations, granting them human characteristics that, in the end, only comfortingly reify the dividing line between human and non-human.

But I also want to distinguish between something fully mechanical/non-organic and a *cyborg* as a transgressive enmeshing of organic and mechanical, because I think something particular is going on when cyborgs are sexualized. Transgression is erotic in itself, often powerfully so, and we tend to construct the blurring of the line between human and non-human as strongly taboo.

Like all sexual taboos, we feel ambivalent toward it, experiencing fear and revulsion at the same time as we're fascinated and deeply attracted by the idea. The art of H.R. Giger blends human, machine, sex, and horror into images of dark eroticism. In David Cronenberg's *Crash*, the experience of bodies pierced and mutilated by technology is made transgressively erotic. He does the same in a slightly different way in *Videodrome* when the protagonist engages in sexual acts with his en-fleshed TV and later becomes a literal fleshly receptacle for a likewise organic videotape. To continue the Cronenberg theme, his son Brandon's *Antiviral* explores the idea of people finding emotionally intense intimacy with their favorite celebrities by being injected with their diseases.

So cyborgian transgressiveness is exactly why we find it so sexy. A sexualized cyborg is at once submissive and potentially dominant, alluring and threatening, subservient and powerful. It is both actual and specific, and abstract and conceptual.

This is where we come back to drones.

Like the sexualized cyborg, a sexualized drone is transgressive, and that transgressiveness is erotic. A drone is not literally an enmeshing of organic and mechanical in the way that a cyborg is, but in terms of power, that's exactly what it is. Although we tend to understand drones in a way that obscures the presence of a human operator, some part of us is aware that the human is still there, their control and surveillance melding with the godlike, inhuman watchfulness of the machine. A drone is also dehumanized state power mingling with abstract technological power, not that the lines between those two are clear at all; indeed, they're connected at the root. If a drone is, in Adam Rothstein's words, "a cultural node–a collection of thoughts, feelings, isolated facts, and nebulous paranoias",[93] then it contains the potential to do violence to accepted boundaries. There's really no way for that to *not* be sexual.

In this sense, drones are cyborgian. But drones are not sexbots. Drones are not subservient in the same way that sexbots are. Drones are nodes for the exercise of social power. *However,* that's not to say that drones aren't subservient at all, because we can't forget about the operator(s). Drones are still created and controlled things, and in that sense there's the potential for the same sexualized relationship that we have with all of our power-laden technologies. Drones are locked in a powerfully intimate relationship with their operators, eyes and hands through which operators do literal and figurative violence to human bodies and watch the aftermath. We even see the same fear that we see in all our tech folklore, of the resistance and rebellion of created things. We talk about drones "going rogue", and we're all very uncomfortable about the idea of combat drones becoming autonomous, even though I think most of us regard it as pretty much inevitable. It's clearly a short step from that to Skynet levels of self-awareness.

This is all to say that we shouldn't just understand drone sexuality in terms of power – though I'd argue that that's probably the most important component – but in terms of *transgression*, and the two are profoundly linked. Drone sexuality is both perverse and normative. It's both dominant and submissive, consensual and nonconsensual. It's both distant and deeply intimate. It's both frightening and arousing, and in fact is arousing *because* it's frightening. Drone sexuality is about both the maintenance of boundaries and their collapse. In that sense, its part and parcel of everything we understand sex to be, and it's also not new. What I argue is new about it is the arrangement of its components and their manifestation. I think drone sexuality has the potential to alter the way we think about sex, what we do with sex, what sex does to us, and how its power works.

Again, I realize that there are a lot of ideas here that aren't anywhere near adequately explored, and a lot that has yet to be teased out. I'm hopeful that this can serve as a beginning that might lead to a larger discussion. Anyway, sex is fun to talk about, regardless. Let's do it.

(Note: After this was written, Robin James followed up with an awesome series of posts[94] [95] responding to and expanding on a lot of what I start fumbling through here. I highly recommend.)

Thirteen Ways of Looking at Livejournal

(as Sarah Wanenchak)

She passes through a sheet of bloody glass. On the other side, she is being born. – Catherynne M. Valente

1.

My self began with words, which were stories.

It's always important to understand that words do not belong to the digital. Nor do they belong to the physical. Words belong to people. People are in both. Nevertheless: my first overt experience of the digital was in words. Words have always been my playthings; I was always a storytelling child. They have always been a means of performance but more for the benefit of myself than anyone else. I have always engaged in a dialogue. *Who am I? What do I want to be today?* We create mythologies with extraordinary explanatory power. We cannot separate ourselves from our stories.

I have words. In the end they are all I have.

A Brief History of the Future

I don't remember my first moment online. That part isn't saved, isn't crystallized, isn't retrievable data. This is not true of everything that came after, and these are things I remember. My first connections with others in this space began with the stories that we told each other, about who we were, what we wanted; I now know that much of this was not true, but you must decide for yourself how important *true* really is.

All of our stories are, to a greater or lesser extent, perfectly true.

From ourselves we created others, or we pulled others from stories that were not ours but which became ours. We created a complex weaving of fiction and roleplaying. We created journals for these characters, for ourselves. We created story-as-interaction; turn by turn we threaded out what we wanted the world to be. Sometimes things slipped out of our control, because our stories are also never truly *ours* once they come into the world. Often this slippage was embarrassing. Overly emotional, too intensely attached. I lost friends when our words meant too much to us, but for so many of us, smashing head-first into adolescence and freshly lonely in new places and new bodies, it was all we had.

Words are fluid. They are slippery. They do not behave. I remember that at some point, my words began to feel genderless. The part of me that consists of bits simply *was*. This was social construction before I knew what social construction meant. Everything I am now comes from the point at which the digital and the physical and I and me and we all together collided in the stupidity that is high school and I had to decide what to do with the pieces.

I have a record of all of this, that I do not read. Sometimes I have to forget that it exists at all. But that never works very well; I can't forget who I am.

2.

We need to believe that *fiction* and *nonfiction* are not the same. We need to believe that *digital* and *physical* are not the same. We need to believe that *online* and *offline* are not the same. We need to believe that *past* and *present* and *future* are not the same. Some of the most heated arguments I had with my parents as a teenager were over whether or not words on a screen actually *meant* anything. Over whether or not I had a right to them.

When we tell ourselves certain stories over and over, it's important to ask why. It's also the question that no one really wants to hear. People have been excommunicated for less.

3.

My handwriting has always been terrible. It's also

painful. Two minutes of it and it's too uncomfortable to continue. I don't hold the pen the right way; perhaps I simply never learned how. The words I produce are often illegible even to me. They don't come fast enough. My brain races ahead and what doesn't hurt is endlessly frustrating. It's like being gagged.

Keyboards gave me my words.

When I was small I would type out nonsense sentences on my father's Kaypro and print them and make him read them aloud, and I would laugh hysterically, because I had the power to create nonsense, which felt like real power indeed. I could disorder the world. Later I ordered myself through a digital conversation that has been going on for the majority of my life.

We had this conversation before the internet, before Livejournal and Blogspot and Facebook and Twitter and Tumblr. The *what* doesn't ever really change. It's the *how* to which we need to pay very close attention. It's the *how* that determines who can converse and who is abandoned to older silences.

4.

I ran away from Facebook. I'm not proud of this. But some of the reason, I think, was that it felt as though it was forcing the river of me into narrow concrete channels. It wasn't letting me *play*.

I am not comfortable with that kind of collapsing of worlds. I contain multitudes. So do we all, but please understand how loud mine are, how I found them, how they grew. I gave them names that had no legal reality. There is nothing more political than the power to self-identify.

I could have found a way to work within it, I think. It wasn't really as narrow as it felt. But sometimes we run because we have to. Sometimes we never find a way to go back.

5.

A cyborg created many masks to amuse themselves, and behind each mask a face came into being, for when we create spaces for things those things are always filled in the end. The masks had power, and through each the cyborg was able to tell a different truth, and all truths were equally true. The cyborg was happy. Also confused. Also contradictory. These were things that had always been so, but now they had solidity and reality; they could be framed in a mirror and seen beyond abstractions.

As the cyborg's faces grew in number, some found this unsettling. *No,* they said. *No, you should have only one. We should only be able to see one. Cast off your other masks and*

give the one that remains a name and wear it always for us so
that we will always know where to look.

Of course the cyborg refused. It couldn't do anything else.

This is not a surprise ending. You already know this story.

6.

I don't read my old Livejournal entries. They are there, I can't delete them, because it feels like dishonesty. But when I summon the courage to look back at any of them, it feels like being skinned alive. I was so raw and foolish; to read the words that came from that person is to be that person again. But of course that person is already me. If we create boundaries where no boundaries were, we lie to ourselves. But please understand that lies are stories which are also real enough to matter.

In those old stories are too many voices. They drown me out. I have locked them away; no one can see them but me and again, I hardly ever look. Like the face of an Old Testament god, I can only see them in fragments before they start to burn out my eyes. It is also true that I live, a little, in fear of discovery.

I also have a paper diary. I never read that either.

7.

The characters I roleplay online have always been men. They have always been the same kinds of men, hurting, looking for someone to fill all the gaps, needing to care and terrified to care in equal parts. When I was very small and lost in worlds of let's-pretend, this was also true. *Let's pretend. Let's pretend that we can be this and we are this and when I talk to this thing that is sometimes you I become more myself. I am faceless but I have avatars that are also me. I build masks and place people behind them. You believe because you want to but also because it's all true.*

I will never be entirely sure whether I was already a transgressor of the gender binary and that's why I told myself the stories I did, or whether the stories I told myself pushed me into transgression. I will never be entirely sure if it makes any difference.

8.

Poetry is not only dream and vision; it is the skeleton architecture of our lives. It lays the foundations for a future of change, a bridge across our fears of what has never been before. – Audre Lorde

Cyborg writing is about the power to survive, not on the basis of original innocence, but on the basis of seizing the

tools to mark the world that marked them as other. – Donna Haraway

9.

I still roleplay. I still inhabit characters that were not born as mine but I make them mine when I wear their masks. One cannot do this with bodies. One has to forget bodies, for a little while. One is still *in* a body, but the body is the interface. The body must disappear.

I am still telling myself stories about myself, about who I was and about who I will be. I can't separate any of this from itself and still make any sense of it at all. I am not internally consistent. I am not sure why I am supposed to be. My body is disciplined but I want to fight this; can words on a screen help me fight this? Where are the master's tools? Did I seize the words or was I given them? How do I move freely within the code when I know the code is not neutral? The code is *never* neutral. The code has never *been* neutral. Someone else sets the rules. We can only do so much to break them.

10.

The cyborg made gods of their masks and tore those

gods down and put them to the fire. The cyborg collapsed their many gods into one god and gifted it a single name, but while others fell down and worshiped this one god, the cyborg could not, because they knew too much to believe.

Every story requires a suspension of disbelief. The cyborg is monotheist, polytheist, atheist. The cyborg recognizes that everything contains a spirit, the cyborg invokes the ghost in the machine and makes of it a digital animism, the cyborg understands that all of this is superstition. The cyborg knows that the world is haunted by many demons. The cyborg is haunted by themselves.

11.

All of this is a frame through which I meet others, myself, the world. Screens, touchpads, numbers, bytes and bits. My eyes; my glasses restrict my field of vision but years ago I stopped being aware of this except at certain times and in certain places. It is the world, now.

I mean *frame* in the social theory sense and I mean *frame* in the sense of: here is something around a picture and the picture is always changing, and: here is a looking glass hung on a wall and everything you see through it is running backwards forever and ever.

But you can, if you wish, step through. Unless you are

already on the other side and looking back at me.

Interfaces are the point and they are also distractions. The best interface is the one that disappears.

12.

The cyborg turned at last and faced themselves, their many-faced self. They opened their arms and embraced each one. Each one was immediate, ever-present, flesh made words and unignorable. They were sharp and as the cyborg danced with them they cut the cyborg's feet to ribbons.

You are all me, the cyborg said. *There is so much pain but I love you.*

13.

I want to believe that the existence of all of these memories and all of that pain and all of that hopeless teenage awkwardness is a net good. That these are stories about myself told to myself that will tell me something about the future. I want to believe in the essential collapse of the temporal. I want to believe in self-integration, and I want to believe that self-integration is never necessary. I want to believe that no one will blame me for any of this. I want to believe that later I won't have to regret anything. I want to believe that all of my digital masks are equally me and that all of my digital ghosts mean me no harm, but that, like all ghosts, they simply have business that remains unfinished.

I don't know if I know too much for this.

I am always turning toward a painful past that becomes a painful present. I am always stepping through the looking glass, I am breaking through the frame. On the other side is always me. This is always true.

I have words. That is enough.

Gravitational Lensing: Death, Twitter, and (Not) Making Sense of it All

(as Sarah Wanenchak)

In preparing to write this post, I found myself going back over Whitney Erin Boesel's post[96] on death and digital/social media mediation, and I found myself running into a lot of the same issues she discusses. She suffered from massive uncertainty regarding how to talk about what she had experienced, or whether to talk about it at all. I'm going through the same. I'm not sure I should even be writing this, or what it will mean when I have. At the same time, I'm not sure how not to write about it, and that in itself is part of what I want to talk about.

Note: this is not going to be particularly organized, or particularly intellectual. It's in part personal Livejournal-esque navel-gazing, part working through some disparate observations regarding how we deal with traumatic life events on social media, part general flailing around. Please bear with me. Or, you know, don't.

Two Fridays ago, I was in New York to take part in a talk/presentation/art installation on video games put on by a collaboration between the Brooklyn Institute for Social Research and the Goethe Institut. I was pumped – it's a topic that anyone who knows me knows I get excited about, and I was looking forward to some awesome discussions, to making new connections and new friends. And then I got a text from my mother telling me to call her immediately. So there I was, sitting in a Roy Rogers in Manhattan in front of a cooling roast beef sandwich with bizarrely loud jazzy R&B on the soundsystem, getting the news that a member of my family had taken his own life.

So that put an interesting spin on the day.

I should note that I've lost family members before, but never someone who wasn't ill and/or elderly. I have been blessed enough to never lose someone like that until now. It was uncharted territory for me. How does one work through news like that? How does one process?

Along with the news, my mother delivered an iron-clad instruction: Do not talk about this on social media. At all. Not yet. Not everyone had been notified.

And the thing is, though I understood and respected and abided by the logic of that, my initial reaction was *what?* because I work through *everything* on social media.

This isn't to say I have no filters at all, because I do. But I'm very forthcoming about what I'm feeling and thinking, to the point of being unprofessional. Since I began using the web in a social way back in junior high school, I've been using it as a sounding board for whatever I'm going through at the time. I put things out there via Facebook, via Twitter (especially Twitter), via my other journaling sites. Increasingly, I do that here. I've been doing it for so long that I don't know how *not* to do it. It's almost impossible for me to process powerful emotion without letting the world know that I'm feeling it.

I clammed up, at least for twenty-four hours or so.

But when I felt like I could reasonably start talking about it publicly – and I did, on Twitter – I found that I had profoundly mixed feelings about doing so. As Whitney noted, social media operates on an attention economy. Was I economizing on my own trauma? Was it my trauma on which to economize? Was I *enjoying* any of the attention I was getting – in the form of outpourings of love and support from my friends and even from mere acquaintances that I want to make it clear I am so, so thankful for.

What the hell *was* I feeling?

I found myself using Twitter as a mirror. I would write whatever I was feeling at the time, post it, look at it for a while and try to work through it from the outside in. I would study my own emotional output in an effort to make it all make sense. Suicide is at once nonsensical and profoundly rational, and as anyone who has ever lost someone that way knows tragically well, it's nearly impossible to reconcile those two things. I was told over and over that *there is no correct way to grieve, there is no right way to go about this, there is no particular thing that you should be feeling* and yet I was gripped by the profound anxiety that I was doing something wrong. Then I would talk about that and try to understand it. Then I would worry about it some more. Now I'm talking about it here, and guess what, I'm *still* worrying.

I think this is what we do. Social media does encourage a kind of self-centeredness by its very nature, but I think it also encourages a deep connection with others – I doubt anyone here would really argue with that at this point – and I think both things are true simultaneously, because I think both things are true of almost all human communication, including just talking to someone else face to face. And how we express ourselves through social media is also how we make sense of ourselves, how we lay out our own narratives, how we explain ourselves to ourselves, even when we don't actually make all that much sense – and we never really do.

But how do we do this? What's appropriate? How should I have talked about this death, how specific should I be? Should I name names, should I detail the method, should I link to his memorial webpage? Whitney came to her own conclusions there, at least sort of:

> It feels as though there is a certain degree of Very
> Close that one should be with someone before one
> steps anywhere near the limelight of their passing, and

while I don't know where the shadows stop and the light begins, I am certain that in that attention is not my place. In a way, new attention is like thermal energy: It flows from where there is more of it to where there is less of it. Were I quite a bit more well known than my friend, then linking would seem appropriate (even though we had long been out of contact): Here, pay attention. Here, help. In 2013, donations of social capital can be made *in memoriam*, too. Under the circumstances, however, I've been at an awkward loss—and unlike when I don't know whether to send flowers or what to wear to a funeral, I can't call my mom up to ask about this one. I don't think any of us know yet. And the questions aren't going away.

I want to talk about him in detail. I want to remember him like this. Social media is increasingly where we go both to remember and to forget, a place that is at once increasingly ephemeral, atemporal, and incredibly bound up in the passage of time. Things happen, people pass in and out of our lives, and we mark their passing this way. We record how they changed us, for better or worse; we understand them through how we lay out their pathways through our own experience. We understand each other. We understand what it means to lose someone, because we look at what we have of them and we know what they meant to us.

Except maybe we don't. Because maybe there isn't any

way to do that at all.

The thing is, we weren't in contact on social media. We weren't Facebook friends. We weren't following each other on Twitter. I don't even know if he *had* a Twitter, though I know he had an Instagram account. So what I found myself dealing with on Twitter was entirely about *me*, entirely about what *I* was going through, and also entirely about this death and this loss almost as an objective fact unconnected to anyone specifically, simply an object out there in the universe like a rock or a star. On Twitter, it felt as if it was coming unmoored, drifting through my timeline without anything to anchor it.

Elaine Scarry wrote a book about pain,[97] and in that book she talked about pain as something unapproachable, something in the face of which all our rationality and all our tools of sense-making break down. In the face of pain we have no language. Like a black hole, we can't see it directly. We can only measure it by what's around it and by what effect it has on other bodies.

His memorial service was livestreamed. I was there. Apparently a lot of people watched. I wonder what that was like, what they were feeling. I wonder if they were posting about it. Before the memorial service, I saw pictures on Twitter of prayer gatherings for him at his school and I broke down crying. I had to fly home before the burial but I saw pictures of his casket on Twitter and I broke down again. The memorial service was a kind of closure but it also felt profoundly unreal. *He* wasn't there. But on Twitter I felt like I got closer.

So my mother said to keep it off social media. What the hell does that even mean? And I still can't bring myself to tell you his name. So all you have to measure his death by is *me*, what I'm telling you about what losing him meant to me. If he's the black hole, I'm the body swinging out toward the event horizon, the pain is Hawking radiation, and none of it really makes any sense ever now.

Death makes no sense, and it doesn't make any more sense on Twitter. But if something like Twitter is the means through which we live a great deal of our lives, then death can't be kept off of it. It finds its way there one way or another. It *is* there. And we look at it, puzzling, trying to approach it and what it means.

But all we see in the end are our own faces.

Sunny Moraine

On Life

Sunny Moraine

Looking into the Heart of Light, the Silence

Colonisation is violence, and there are many ways to carry out that violence. – Philip Gourevitch

It's no small thing that I quote from Philip Gourevitch's harrowing book *We Wish to Inform You That Tomorrow We Will Be Killed With Our Families* at the beginning of my story in *We See a Different Frontier*, "A Heap of Broken Images". Read in a summer off from college, it's a book that has stayed with me in all the years since. Some of it is naturally the sheer horror of the subject matter – wrenching and vivid without feeling prurient, the descriptions of the Rwandan genocide nevertheless slotted neatly into a blood-soaked part of me that has been there since I was very small. I think this is part of why I wrote the story that I did and part of why I continue to write the stories that I do – I'm fascinated by evil, and the evil that most fascinates me is not supernatural in origin but evil in all its everyday mundane banality, the fundamentally casual nature of an attempt to erase an entire people. Supernatural evil always seemed to me like a cop-out, a way to avoid the real problem.

So as a child I was fascinated by the Holocaust. I

devoured books, though somehow I never had the strength for films; books were approachable and at the same time immensely more horrific, a kind of horror that I could soak in without the onslaught of images. And yet there were images too; in middle school I discovered Art Spiegelman's *Maus* and Keiji Nakazawa's *Barefoot Gen,* and my fascination with mass death expanded into the practice of warfare itself. These images were somehow a middle ground between film and prose – I could still use them to approach the truth, to go into dark places.

It was probably at this point that I began to intuit the second thing that has lingered with me long after finishing Gourevitch's book: the inability to approach the truly evil, the desolate tyranny of silence that reigns when we run out of words – or can't find them at all. We tell stories as a way to, in the words of Douglas Adams, "sidle up to the problem sideways when it's not looking" but in the end it always sees us, and we look back, struck dumb.

It shouldn't escape us, then: the violence inherent not only in silence but in words, not only in seeing but in being seen. Colonialism is an orgy of violence in every sense, violence physical, psychological, emotional, cultural, environmental. All colonialism is, to a greater or lesser extent, a kind of genocide in that the ultimate aim is to cripple or destroy an entire people; all too often throughout history it has been devastatingly effective. It's a violence that is also fundamentally *atemporal:* as culture and history are erased, the past is destroyed, with the loss of the past, there is no sense to be made of the present, and without the past or the present the future becomes mutilated and distorted. It's not enough to call these effects scars, because a scar only becomes a scar when it has healed – it would be more accurate to describe them as rips in the fabric of reality itself, bloody gashes through which something horrible creeps. It's too simplistic to say that "violence begets violence" – violence *is* violence and violence devours everything. Violence erases meaning.

Years later, early in my graduate studies, I encountered Elaine Scarry's *The Body in Pain*, another book that's stayed with me. In the book's first section, Scarry draws distinctions and connections between warfare and torture, and makes the point that nuclear war is where the lines become hopelessly blurred. Beginning with a singular devastating event, the effects of a nuclear strike don't end with the fallout; as I had already learned from Nakazawa, the effects go on and on for years, lingering in cells and psyches, destroying lives long after the conflict itself is over. Scarry talks as if nuclear war was unique in this respect.

But I think we know it's not.

How do we talk about this? Where do we find the words?

What I was trying to do in "A Heap of Broken Images" was not to approach the unapproachable but instead to capture the impossibility of approach. My main character, Shairoven, struggles to make sense of the massacre perpetrated on her people by human colonists, and she does it within the context of a culture that makes this nearly impossible – literally without words to describe the feelings of rage and loss that accompany such an atrocity, there is nothing to say about it. The humans themselves certainly don't help matters, with their empty gestures and their clumsy attempts at owning what they've done while declaring that it's all right now and clearly *it will never happen again.* They study the killing as if it were something separate from themselves, as if they were impartial and unconnected observers.

One of the story's early scenes is nearly lifted wholesale from what was, for me, one of the most devastating images from Gourevitch's book, where the bones of the dead are viewed where they've fallen in a classroom, scattered and clean and strangely lovely:

> The dead at Nyarubuye were, I'm afraid, beautiful.
> There was no getting around it. The skeleton is a
> beautiful thing. The randomness of the fallen forms,
> the strange tranquility of their rude exposure, the skull
> here, the arm bent in some uninterpretable gesture
> there – these things were beautiful, and their beauty
> only added to the affront of the place. I couldn't settle
> on any meaningful response: revulsion, alarm, sorrow,
> grief, shame, incomprehension, sure, but nothing truly
> meaningful. I just looked, and I took photographs,
> because I wondered whether I could really see what I
> was seeing while I saw it, and I also wanted an excuse

to look a bit more closely.

We went through the first room and out the far side. There was another room and another and another and another. They were all full of bodies, and more bodies were scattered in the grass, which was thick and wonderfully green. Standing outside, I heard a crunch. The old Canadian colonel stumbled in front of me, and I saw, though he did not notice, that his foot had rolled on a skull and broken it. For the first time at Nyarubuye my feelings focused, and what I felt was a small but keen anger at this man. Then I heard another crunch, and felt a vibration underfoot. I had stepped on one, too.

In "A Heap of Broken Images", what makes confronting the massacre so difficult for us as humans is that we face our own complicity, and our first and strongest instinct is to escape self-incrimination. But there are the bones and there are the broken skulls, and we can't help but look. And here am I, a white Westerner, existing in the context of a society wherein I have benefited indirectly but greatly from colonialism as an ongoing historical process, as real violence done to real people who I will never meet. So I consider the humans in my story and I think that maybe they shouldn't say anything at all. Maybe their task – and it's the most difficult task in many ways, not that they deserve sympathy – is to listen.

And here is where I perceive a flaw in the story:

Shairoven and her people don't speak about the massacre because they lack the words, but the words were not taken away from them by the colonizers; they never had them to begin with. I am sitting here in a world in which my people have stolen words, violated words, erased words, and left our victims to scream into the tyranny of that silence, unheard.

It is possible to use stories to break that silence. They might be one of the few things that can.

Like Wheat that Springeth Green

Nothing worth doing is completed in our lifetime; therefore, we are saved by hope. Nothing true or beautiful or good makes complete sense in any immediate context of history; therefore, we are saved by faith. Nothing we do, however virtuous, can be accomplished alone; therefore, we are saved by love. – Reinhold Niebuhr

I don't know how comfortable I am calling myself a Christian anymore. That's less to do with me than with other Christians – though I think we might, rather than running away from the word, be better served by taking back from the people who have been doing reprehensible things with it for so long – but it's also me. I don't really go to church anymore. I don't even pray all that often. I like prayer, I like the idea of prayer, and I enjoy it when I do it. But I've lost the habit. I've lost a lot of things. I think I am, as Anne Lamott has put it, a "Jesusy Person" – down with the man himself, in love with a lot of the theology, and – even if continuously full of doubt – at least trying to live as if the major points are true, because you know what, I need to. But troubled by the rest of it, by the part of it that can be properly called the kingdom of this world, and separated from it as a result.

But regardless of what I am or am not comfortable calling myself or thinking of myself as, today leading into this weekend is major. Christmas gets all the attention, but this, right here, this is the big three-day thing. This is what it all comes down to. This is what we've all been gearing up for, and more, *this is where we begin to understand what kind of story we're in.* Christmas gives us a glimpse of that, and regardless of whether or not you believe in any element of Christianity, it's still a pretty amazing story: a special, holy thing comes into being in the most unlikely place, to the most unlikely people. A teenage mother, a confused father, a bunch of outcast drunks, some animals, and a terrifying chorus line of angels. That's the first hint of what kind of (profoundly *weird*) story this is.

There are a lot of other hints along the way. Jesus is continuously dropping them. Some of them are a lot more than hints – some of them are him trying to get his tremendously clueless disciples to just *get it* already. *Okay,* he says, and I can almost see him rolling his eyes. *Okay, so that didn't work. How about you look at it this way…No? Still? Man, this is gonna be a long couple years.*

But then we get to tonight, and the story seems like it's headed for the worst possible ending. The hero is dying, in one of the most agonizing and most shameful ways imaginable. His friends have abandoned him to their own terror and stupidity. Love is losing and power is winning.

Justice seems like a bad joke, and hope like the pointless dream of a hopeless fool.

Fred Clark observes the poignant fact[98] that the story of the crucifixion and its aftermath is basically the story of the world so far. We're in the middle of that, that awful moment. We're stuck in a perpetual Saturday, with the wretchedness of Friday all around us, and little hope of anything better to come:

> And to be honest, it doesn't seem terribly likely, because Saturday, this Saturday, is all we've ever known. Yesterday was this same Saturday, and so was the day before that, and the day before that, and the day before that.
>
> Why should we expect that tomorrow will be any different?
>
> Seriously, just look around. Does it *look* like the meek are inheriting the earth? Does it look like those who hunger and thirst for justice are being filled? Does it look like the merciful are being shown mercy?
>
> Jesus was meek and merciful and hungry for justice and look where that got *him*. They killed him. We killed him. Power won.
>
> That's what this everyday Saturday shows us — power *always* wins. "If you want a picture of the future," George Orwell wrote, "imagine a boot

stomping on a human face — forever."

But I want to believe in Sunday.

I think what this too often means for some is that all
we have to do is *wait* – the big Whoever has it all taken
care of, so we can sit back and just be here when Sunday
comes. (In the meantime, let's make sure we say the right
nasty things about all the bad people, because if *they're*
hanging around when Sunday comes... hoo, boy.)

But Christ never says that. He says the exact opposite.
Christ promises justice, mercy, the death of power and the
eternal reign of love, but he never, *ever* gives people that
kind of out. Waiting isn't enough. Sitting on your hands
and pretending to be better than everyone else because
you think and say the right things makes you a
whitewashed tomb. You want justice? Fight injustice. You
want freedom? See the captives freed. You want mercy? Be
merciful. You want love? Love. Sunday comes when you
work for it, when you *do*. The doing matters. First that.
Then Sunday. Get through Saturday as best you can. But
above all, keep moving.

But what am I feeling on Saturday?

A while ago, I wrote about anger, about writing in
anger, about writing in a state of ugly rage. I wrote about
finding the poison inside yourself and letting it out into
your words, about using it to tell all the truths you've ever
been told to hide. About how, when your heart is a

volcano and these things are burning through your skin, to let them out and make them a light. Because I also wrote about courage, and I wrote about hope, because without those two, rage is just rage.

And ultimately, on its own, rage can't save us.

I can't speak for anyone else, and I wouldn't try to. I'm just wise enough now to know that there is no one best way for everyone, no single right path to walk. But when *I'm* here in my Saturday, and I'm hurt, angry, frightened, and full of despair, this is the story I come back to. It may be true. It might not be. What I do know is there are things in it that can save me, because rage isn't all there is, because hope is waiting there at the end of it if I have the courage to find it. Everything seems lost a lot of the time. Everything seems pointless. Everything seems like a bad joke, and I don't like the kind of story it seems like this is.

But we can't really know what kind of story we're in until it ends.

And but so, this is why we hope for Sunday and why we live for the hope of Sunday. Even though we can't know for sure that Sunday will ever come and even if Saturday is all we ever get to see.

Life Like a Pin

I found out that Dermatillomania and Dermatophagia had names almost two decades after I started picking off and eating my own skin.

It was all kinds of skin, in all kinds of places. Cuticles, the pads of my fingers, my feet, my head, anywhere there were scabs or bites or any imperfection in the skin. I learned very early in my life that I enjoyed the taste of my own blood. I enjoyed the iron and the slightly spicy tang, the way old, dried blood crunches between the teeth.

Did you know that the skin on the bottoms of your feet has a rubbery texture when chewed? It's a little like slightly dry squid, or maybe more like beef jerky. It's pleasant. Everything about the process of Dermatophagia is pleasant. The taste is pleasant, the pain is pleasant, the feeling of stress drifting away is deeply pleasant. The scars are less pleasant, as is the inability to explain to your classmates and teachers why you're digging holes in your legs with paper clips.

This is disgusting, isn't it? That's the thing about these two deeply interconnected disorders: they are irredeemably disgusting. There is nothing attractive about them. They can't be twisted around to be fun and amusing and quirky like popular culture has done with Obsessive-Compulsive Disorder – and what it's done is its own kind of disgusting, but let's leave that alone for now. Dermatillomania and Dermatophagia cannot be made palatable – if you'll excuse a very bad pun – to the people who don't live with them. You can't make an inspirational movie about an artist who carves pits into her arms and devours the scabs. You can't have a fun show about a detective who has no skin left around his fingernails. You can't have a manic pixie dreamgirl who makes a snack out of her own dried blood.

I want to be clear about something: these disorders are not what we think of when we think of "self-injuring". They are not about depression or anger, at least not in the same way, though it's not uncommon for people doing this stuff to also be depressed and/or angry. The act of picking and consuming one's own flesh can have a profoundly stress-relieving component, but unlike the compulsions associated with OCD, most of us with Dermatophagia and Dermatillomania find our symptoms pleasurable while they're occurring. The shame, confusion, and self-disgust are less pleasurable, but when you're actually in the middle of it, you're thinking about nothing but how much you enjoy it, and the shame and pain that you know will follow aren't enough to keep you from wanting to do it. I'm familiar with the difference between these categories of compulsion, because I also had intense

OCD-related compulsions as a child (they're much better now, though they stick around in various forms) and there was *nothing* fun about them. Every aspect of them was unremittingly awful and all I wanted was to be able, finally, to stop.

Writing about this hurts. It opens up a lot of old wounds. As a child I was tortured for it – I tortured myself for fun and then other kids did the same thing to me for the same reason. I hear about kids who were picked on for being fat or smart or gay, and it feels like some kind of petty version of the Oppression Olympics but you have no idea how much I wish those had been my primary problems, because I think I could have gotten over the shame of those things so much more easily. Again: *you can't redeem this, you can't make it inspiring.* It's just sad and gross and ugly. And now, years later, I have scars all over my body and I still have symptoms and I'm still not sure how to admit to people that this is a facet of my daily experience of existence.

Giving it a name helped. In folklore it's a common idea that giving a demon a name gives you a degree of power over it, and when a disorder has a name, it means two things: it's not your fault, and you're not alone. But when it's something like this, there's only so much that naming the demon can do. The average person who sees you displaying visible symptoms, or the evidence of them, probably won't respond well to the explanation that you have a brain disorder. You're that freak with ugly hands who picks at themselves all the time. And if you're like me and you can hide the symptoms well enough that they aren't usually very visible, you'll still never stop being that kid who couldn't hide what they were doing any more than someone at the worst level of drug addiction can hide the fact that they're using.

Why am I writing about this now? I've been trying to for a while, and have made some sporadic, moderately successful attempts. Some of it is the hope that I might educate people, some of it is a desire to let anyone dealing with this know that they aren't alone, but a lot of it is that writing is where I Deal With My Shit. It's a safe space. Or it should be.

But the fact is, I haven't dealt with My Shit the way I want to. I haven't been able to bring it into my fiction, and I think that needs to happen. Something always stops me at the last moment, though I haven't worked out exactly what – it's not conscious, whatever it is. It's not fear or resistance that I'm directly aware of. Regardless, I really do believe what Anne Lamott says about bringing your own ugliness and pain into your writing:

> Maybe you feel that Wordsworth was right, maybe Rumi, maybe Stephen Mitchell writing on Job: "The physical body is acknowledged as dust, the personal drama as delusion. It is as if the world we perceive through our senses, that whole gorgeous and terrible pageant, were the breath-thin surface of a bubble, and everything else, inside and outside, is pure radiance.

Both suffering and joy come then like a brief reflection, and death like a pin."

But you can't get to any of these truths by sitting in a field smiling beatifically, avoiding your anger and damage and grief. Your anger and damage and grief are the way to the truth. We don't have much truth to express unless we have gone into those rooms and closets and woods and abysses that we were told not go in to. When we have gone in and looked around for a long while, just breathing and finally taking it in – then we will be able to speak in our own voice and to stay in the present moment. And that moment is home.

I think so many of us write because we're angry and damaged and grieving, because everyone is, and because we all have this crazy idea that somewhere at some point in the past we were home and then that home was taken away from us, and we're trying to get back there, except we're also trying to describe it to ourselves so we know it when we see it, and on some level we know that the only way through that is deeply and profoundly painful, like being born. It takes immense courage, courage that a lot of us just straight up don't have, and I don't think there's any shame in that.

But I'm trying to get to my anger and my damage and my grief and make something beautiful out of it, or at least something powerful. I'm trying to take that disgusting, irredeemable thing in my past and my present and most likely my future and redeem it, at least a little. I'm angry at the kids who picked me out as a living symbol of everything they hated and feared and didn't want be, and I'm angry at the adults who did nothing to stop them. I'm hurt by that, more deeply than I can say, and I carry the scars of that hurt on my body, in the skin I tore open over and over again. I hurt for the other kids who grew up doing what I did and didn't understand or know how to stop, and were therefore utterly alone in what they were going through. And I'm grieving for the child I was, who suffered in a way that is senselessly and incomprehensibly ugly. Not even ugly in an impressive, TV movie kind of way. Just small and gross. Insignificant. Something to be mocked and forgotten.

Believe me: it was very significant, and I don't have the luxury of forgetting it.

I need to write about the things that seem irredeemable. I need to stop running away and find a way to make some kind of art out of all the things of which I'm so profoundly ashamed, even art of the most mutilated kind. So here's a resolution for 2014: I'm going to write my damage. I'm going to find a way. And it's going to hurt, and I don't think it's going to get me home, but I do think it might at least result in some decent stories.

Sometimes that's about the best you can hope for.

All That We See or Seem

Two things happened in the last month. The first is that I came out to my students – gender-wise, and my unconformity. The second is that I wrote a thing for my department's newsletter about social media and how I use it. I didn't realize those how connected those things were until about ten minutes ago.

There's a third thing that I think might be behind most of that connection, which is that I will not be receiving funding next year. That in itself isn't necessarily something to be angry about – I got more than a lot of grad students get, nationwide – but how it happened was, without going into detail, less than satisfactory, and I've been doing some major reevaluating about my place here and my relationship with this institution and what it all means to me personally. And what started as real anger has turned into a kind of freedom I didn't expect.

I don't care anymore.

Which, ironically, might mean that I can actually care about the right things for the first time in my entire graduate school career.

A Brief History of the Future

So I came out to my students. I explained what "genderqueer" meant, and then I put myself up there as an example. I did it mostly in passing – an "and I'm that, so you know what that is already" – but it felt big.

It's not the first time I've come out to a class, and it wasn't the first time this semester where I used myself as an example. I'm a weird confluence of identity categories, exactly like most people: white, middle/upper middle class in many respects but growing up in a lower middle class neighborhood on a lower middle class income, born with a female body but not identifying that way in terms of my gender, sexually sort of all over the place, able-bodied but possessing a wacky constellation of mental illnesses, disorders, and cognitive disabilities. Whatever, nobody's normal, we all agreed. There's no such thing.

I had not yet been informed that I wouldn't be funded. Maybe some part of me knew already that this semester was different.

It's always an interesting question, how much of yourself you reveal to a class. How much of yourself you reveal to yourself. Coming out to someone about anything strange or uncomfortable makes that person into kind of a mirror; see yourself through their eyes and suddenly you might see something different. It might not be *true*, but it's there. In my mid-twenties I came to an understanding of myself as genderqueer, but I've never been comfortable with gender, and I've never been comfortable with my body, and I've always felt like my mind was actively trying to hurt me. I'm not comfortable with anything. At all. Ever. But life has become a process of getting to be Okay with that, and talking about it to other people is part of how I've been getting there.

So then I wasn't funded, and while I've been decoupling from Giving A Shit since my comprehensive exams, this finally kicked me away completely.

Abruptly I was saying everything. I was just talking. I told them a lot, in private and in the classroom itself. My final class, I sat on a table in front of my students and I told them the story of the last few weeks. I told them I wouldn't be teaching again in the fall and how sad that made me. I told them how angry I was. I told them about how diseased higher education is, and about how increasingly their own institutions are cheating them. And I told them what I had realized, after many conversations with wise people: We don't have to stay here. We don't have to chain ourselves to failing institutions. We can make space elsewhere for the work we want to do. For some of us it's easy and for some of us it's so much harder, but we have to try. Those of us with power have to step back and empower others. It's painful, this kind of self-confrontation.

But it was more painful to keep lying to them, and lying by omission is still a lie.

I've made 2014 the year I started writing my rage, and

now I'm making it the year I stopped lying and started talking. I'm making this space aggressively, with my fists and my fingernails and my feet, with my tongue and my teeth. I'm learning how to live in my body. I'm working on not being afraid anymore.

I wrote this for the newsletter, among other things:

> We're taught that we're not supposed to do that, to be vulnerable. Life teaches us this, but I think academia teaches it especially hard. When you're in graduate school you're highly susceptible to fear—What's going to happen to me? Am I going to find a job? What do all these faculty think of me? How am I coming off? Does so and so hate me? Am I letting people down? *Oh God*. That kind of fear can break you, but keeping it inside for even greater fear of looking weak makes it even worse, and at some point I decided I couldn't do that anymore.

It's more terrifying for me, now, to continue to pretend I'm not terrified. So I'm going to stop. I'm going to dare to be a human being in the most public of ways. We'll see what happens.

~

Sometimes, when I'm in a certain place in my head, I imagine slicing my chest open with a boxcutter. Somehow it's sharp enough to pierce the sternum, and I pull my ribcage apart with my bare hands. A flock of crows explodes into the air. There's never any blood. Inside I'm smooth and clean and full of whispering birds.

A Brief History of the Future

Endnotes

1 Chris Friend, "Writing as a Cyborg Act", 04 November 2012
http://chrisfriend.us/Blog/files/writing-as-cyborgian.php

2 Chris Friend, "Writing as a Cyborg Act", 04 November 2012
http://chrisfriend.us/Blog/files/writing-as-cyborgian.php

3 Chris Friend, "Writing as a Cyborg Act", 04 November 2012
http://chrisfriend.us/Blog/files/writing-as-cyborgian.php

4 Chris Friend, "Writing as a Cyborg Act", 04 November 2012
http://chrisfriend.us/Blog/files/writing-as-cyborgian.php

5 Chris Friend, "Writing as a Cyborg Act", 04 November 2012
http://chrisfriend.us/Blog/files/writing-as-cyborgian.php

6 Adam Rothstein, "How to Write Drone Fiction", *The State,* 20 January
2013 http://www.thestate.ae/how-to-write-drone-fiction/

7 Sarah Wanenchak, "Digital Dualism and Stories of the Real",
Cyborgology, 24 May 2012
http://thesocietypages.org/cyborgology/2012/05/24/digital-dualism-
and-stories-of-the-real/

8 Sarah Wanenchak, "No One Tells Stories Alone", *Cyborgology,* 15
September 2012
http://thesocietypages.org/cyborgology/2012/09/15/no-one-tells-
stories-alone/

9 Nathan Jurgenson, "Digital Dualism versus Augmented Reality",
Cyborgology, 24 February 2011
http://thesocietypages.org/cyborgology/2011/02/24/digital-dualism-
versus-augmented-reality/

10 Richard Carroll, "The Trouble with History and Fiction", *M/C Journal,* Vol. 14, No. 3, 2011. http://journal.media-culture.org.au/index.php/mcjournal/article/viewArticle/372/0

11 Gary Allen Fine, *Shared Fantasy: Role Playing Games as Social Worlds.* 2002. Chicago: University of Chicago Press

12 Sarah Wanenchak, "Tags, Threads, and Frames: Toward a Synthesis of Interaction Ritual and Livejournal Roleplaying", *Game Studies*, Vol. 10, No. 1, 2010. http://gamestudies.org/1001/articles/wanenchak

13 Jeremy Antley, "No Accidents, Comrade", *The New Inquiry,* 17 August 2012. http://thenewinquiry.com/essays/no-accidents-comrade/

14 Christopher Franklin, "Spec Ops: The Line", 19 August 2012 http://www.errantsignal.com/blog/?p=342

15 Olivia Rosane, "The Community of Story", *The State*, 7 September 2012 http://www.thestate.ae/the-community-of-story/

16 Jenny Davis, "Re-integrating the Self Narrative", *Cyborgology,* 18 December 2011 http://thesocietypages.org/cyborgology/2011/12/28/re-integrating-the-self-narrative/

17 Jenny Davis, "Curating Reality", *Cyborgology*, 30 April 2012 http://thesocietypages.org/cyborgology/2012/04/30/curating-reality/

18 Whitney Erin Boesel, "Meaning-Making Through Numbers: Emotional Self-Quantification", *Cyborgology,* 13 September 2012 http://thesocietypages.org/cyborgology/2012/09/13/meaning-making-through-numbers-emotional-self-quantification/

19 Interview, *Bill Moyers Journal*, 17 April 2009 http://www.pbs.org/moyers/journal/04172009/watch.html

20 John Scalzi, "Writer, Professional, Good", 28 January 2012
http://whatever.scalzi.com/2012/01/28/writer-professional-good/

21 Anne Lamott, *Bird by Bird: Some Instructions on Writing and Life*. 1995.
New York: Anchor

22 Sam Byers, "The End of Everything: Fiction's Fretful Futures", *The
Weeklings*, 10 January 2013
http://www.theweeklings.com/sbyers/2013/01/10/the-end-of-the-end-
of-everything-fictions-fretful-futures-part-i/

23 Toby Litt, "The Reader and Technology", *Granta*, 12 April 2012
http://www.granta.com/New-Writing/The-Reader-And-Technology

24 Am Sonntag, "Technology, the Internet, and Literature", 17 February
2013 http://amsonntag.wordpress.com/2013/02/17/technology-the-
internet-and-literature/

25 Teresa Nielsen Hayden, "Slushkiller", *Making Light*, 02 February 2004
http://nielsenhayden.com/makinglight/archives/004641.html

26 William Horwood, *Dunction Wood*. 1985. London: Arrow Books

27 Sean Williams, "The Cuckoo", *Clarkesworld*, No. 91, April 2014

28 David A. Banks, "On Performative Internet Memes: Planking,
Owling, and Stocking", *Cyborgology*, 21 September 2011
http://thesocietypages.org/cyborgology/2011/09/21/on-performative-
internet-memes-planking-owling-stocking/

29 Jenny Davis, "Internet Memes: The Mythology of Augmented
Society", *Cyborgology*, 06 December 2011
http://thesocietypages.org/cyborgology/2011/12/06/internet-memes-
the-mythology-of-augmented-society/

30 PJ Rey, "The Cyborgology of *Blade Runner*", *Cyborgology.* 21 May 2011 http://thesocietypages.org/cyborgology/2011/05/21/the-cyborgology-of-blade-runner/

31 PJ Rey, "How Cyberpunk Warned Against Apple's Consumer Revolution", *Cyborgology*, 01 December 2011 http://thesocietypages.org/cyborgology/2011/12/01/how-cyberpunk-warned-against-apples-consumer-revolution/

32 Sunny Moraine, "Speculative Fiction, Atemporality, and Augmented Reality", *Cyborgology*, 26 May 2011 http://thesocietypages.org/cyborgology/2011/05/26/speculative-fiction-atemporality-and-augmented-reality/

33 Dave Paul Strohecker, "The Zombie in Film", *Cyborgology*, 27 February 2012 http://thesocietypages.org/cyborgology/2012/02/27/the-zombie-in-film-full-essay-parts-i-ii-and-iii/

34 Catherynne M. Valente, *Silently and Very Fast.* 2012. Stirling, NJ: Wyrm Publishing

35 PJ Rey, "There is no 'Cyberspace'", *Cyborgology*, 01 February 2012 http://thesocietypages.org/cyborgology/2012/02/01/there-is-no-cyberspace/

36 Anne Lamott, *Bird by Bird: Some Instructions on Writing and Life.* 1995. New York: Anchor

37 Sunny Moraine, "So Sharp That Blood Must Flow", *Lightspeed*, No. 49, June 2014 http://www.lightspeedmagazine.com/fiction/so-sharp-that-blood-must-flow/

38 Stephan Totilo, "An Ordinary Life, an Extraordinary Death, and the Video Game That Wasn't Meant to Be", *Kotaku*, 12 March 2012 http://kotaku.com/5892375/a-normal-life-an-extraordinary-death-and-

the-video-game-that-wasnt-meant-to-be

39 Michael Rougeau, "Most people aren't interested in Windows 8, massive survey finds", *Tech Radar,* 15 November 2012 http://www.techradar.com/us/news/software/operating-systems/most-people-arent-interested-in-windows-8-massive-survey-finds-1112964

40 Nathan Jurgenson, "Apertures Matter (a brief response to "Stories in Focus"), *Cyborgology,* 27 August 2012 http://thesocietypages.org/cyborgology/2012/08/27/apertures-matter-a-brief-response-to-stories-in-focus/

41 Sarah Wanenchak, "Stories in Focus:Visual media, style, and documentation", *Cyborgology,* 25 August 2012 http://thesocietypages.org/cyborgology/2012/08/25/stories-in-focus-visual-media-style-and-documentation/

42 Tom Bissell, "Thirteen Ways of Looking at a Shooter", *Grantland,* 12 July 2012 http://grantland.com/features/line-explores-reasons-why-play-shooter-games/

43 Brendan Keogh, *Killing is Harmless: A Critical Reading of Spec Ops: The Line.* 2013. Stolen Projects

44 Jesper Juul, *Half Real: Video Games Between Real Rules and Fictional Worlds.* 2005. Cambridge: The MIT Press

45 Steven Poole, "Working for the Man", 27 October 2008 http://stevenpoole.net/articles/working-for-the-man/

46 David A. Banks, "The Parable of the Coffee Maker and the Design Sir", *Cyborgology,* 20 January 2014 http://thesocietypages.org/cyborgology/2014/01/20/the-parable-of-the-coffee-maker-and-the-design-sir/

47 Christopher Franklin, "The Last of Us", 22 July 2013
    http://www.errantsignal.com/blog/?p=525

48 Entertainment Software Association, "Industry Facts",
    http://www.theesa.com/facts/index.asp

49 Luke Plunkett, "Some Idiots Wanted to Move the Girl on the Cover of
    The Last of Us", *Kotaku*, 12 December 2012
    http://kotaku.com/5968027/some-idiots-wanted-to-take-a-girl-off-the-
    cover-of-the-last-of-us

50 Jeremy Antley, "Ephemerality is a Snap...", 03 February 2013
    http://www.peasantmuse.com/2013/02/ephemerality-is-snap.html

51 Nathan Jurgenson, "Pics and it Didn't Happen", *The New Inquiry*, 07
    February 2013 http://thenewinquiry.com/essays/pics-and-it-didnt-
    happen/

52 Sarah Wanenchak, "The Atemporality of Ruin Porn: The Carcass and
    the Ghost", *Cyborgology*, 16 May 2012
    http://thesocietypages.org/cyborgology/2012/05/16/the-atemporality-
    of-ruin-porn-the-carcass-the-ghost/

53 Sarah Wanenchak, "Books in Ruins: Ebooks, temporality, and
    tension", *Cyborgology*, 02 November 2012
    http://thesocietypages.org/cyborgology/2012/11/02/books-in-ruins-
    ebooks-temporality-and-tension/

54 Jenny Davis, "In Snapchat We Trust", *Cyborgology*, 12 February 2013
    http://thesocietypages.org/cyborgology/2013/02/12/in-snapchat-we-
    trust/

55 Robinson Meyer, "@Horse_ebooks is the Most Successful Piece of
    Cyber Fiction, Ever", *The Atlantic*, 24 September 2013
    http://www.theatlantic.com/technology/archive/2013/09/-horse-

ebooks-is-the-most-successful-piece-of-cyber-fiction-ever/279946/

56 Daniel Sinker, "Eulogy for a Horse", 24 September 2013
http://dansinker.com/post/62183207705/eulogy-for-a-horse

57 Alex Hern, "The truth behind one YouTube account's 77,000
mysterious videos", *The Guardian*, 01 May 2014
http://www.theguardian.com/technology/shortcuts/2014/may/01/trut
h-youtube-mysterious-videos-webdriver-torso

58 David A. Banks, "Our Emotional Attachment to Interfaces",
Cyborgology, 01 June 2012
http://thesocietypages.org/cyborgology/2012/06/01/our-emotional-
attachment-to-interfaces/

59 Nathan Jurgenson, "The Data Self: (A Dialectic)", *Cyborgology*, 30
January 2012 http://thesocietypages.org/cyborgology/2012/01/30/the-
data-self-a-dialectic/

60 Jenny Davis, "The High Cost of Abstention", *Cyborgology*, 06 March
2012 http://thesocietypages.org/cyborgology/2012/03/06/the-high-
cost-of-abstention/

61 Whitney Erin Boesel, "A New Privacy, Pt. 1: Distributed Agency and
the Myth of Autonomy", *Cyborgology*, 21 May 2012
http://thesocietypages.org/cyborgology/2012/05/21/a-new-privacy-pt-
i-distributed-agency-the-myth-of-autonomy/

62 Nathan Jurgenson, "Glad I Didn't Have Facebook in High School!",
Cyborgology, 26 November 2012
http://thesocietypages.org/cyborgology/2012/11/26/glad-i-didnt-have-
facebook-in-high-school/

63 Jenny Davis, "Structuring Identity Prosumption", *Cyborgology*, 27
November 2012

http://thesocietypages.org/cyborgology/2012/11/27/structuring-identity-prosumption/

64 Rob Horning, "Everyday schadenfreude", *The New Inquiry*, 27 November 2012 http://thenewinquiry.com/blogs/marginal-utility/everydayschadenfreude/

65 Whitney Erin Boesel, "Let Sleeping Memories Lie: High School and the Facebookless Past", 28 November 2012 http://thesocietypages.org/cyborgology/2012/11/28/let-sleeping-memories-lie-high-school-and-the-facebookless-past/

66 Michael Sacasas, "Memory, Facebook, and the Narrative Unity of a Life", 29 November 2012 http://thefrailestthing.com/2012/11/29/memory-facebook-and-the-narrative-unity-of-a-life/

67 Sarah Wanenchak, "Thirteen Ways of Looking at Livejournal", *Cyborgology*, 29 November 2012 http://thesocietypages.org/cyborgology/2012/11/29/thirteen-ways-of-looking-at-livejournal/

68 Whitney Erin Boesel, "What's in a (User)Name?", *Cyborgology*, 24 July 2013 http://thesocietypages.org/cyborgology/2013/07/24/whats-in-a-username/

69 Nathan Jurgenson, "Glad I Didn't Have Facebook in High School!", *Cyborgology*, 26 November 2012 http://thesocietypages.org/cyborgology/2012/11/26/glad-i-didnt-have-facebook-in-high-school/

70 Nathan Jurgenson, "Victim Blaming: How Not to Teach Students About Privacy", *Cyborgology*, 27 June 2013 http://thesocietypages.org/cyborgology/2013/06/27/victim-blaming-

how-not-to-teach-students-about-privacy/

71 Cory Doctorow, "The Coming Civil War over General Purpose Computing", *BoingBoing*, 08 August 2012 http://boingboing.net/2012/08/23/civilwar.html

72 PJ Rey, "How Cyberpunk Warned Against Apple's Consumer Revolution", *Cyborgology*, 01 December 2011 http://thesocietypages.org/cyborgology/2011/12/01/how-cyberpunk-warned-against-apples-consumer-revolution/

73 Jaron Lanier, *You Are Not a Gadget: A Manifesto*. 2010. New York: Knopf

74 Joann Greco, "The Psychology of Ruin Porn", *CityLab*, 06 January 2012 http://www.citylab.com/design/2012/01/psychology-ruin-porn/886/

75 Sarah Wanenchak, "Michael Chrisman's Long Now", *Cyborgology*, 04 January 2012 http://thesocietypages.org/cyborgology/2012/01/04/michael-chrismans-long-now/

76 Nathan Jurgenson, "The Faux-Vintage Photo", *Cyborgology*, 14 May 2011 http://thesocietypages.org/cyborgology/2011/05/14/the-faux-vintage-photo-full-essay-parts-i-ii-and-iii/

77 Nathan Jurgenson, "The Faux-Vintage Photo Part II: Grasping for Authenticity", *Cyborgology*, 11 May 2011 http://thesocietypages.org/cyborgology/2011/05/11/the-faux-vintage-photo-part-ii-grasping-for-authenticity/

78 Will Viney, "The Ruins of the Future: An Extract", 30 August 2010 http://narratingwaste.wordpress.com/2010/08/30/ruins-of-the-future-an-extract/

79 RD, "Heterotopia, the soul of ruins in Vincent J. Stoker", *Les Photographes,* 07 November 2011 http://www.lesphotographes.com/old-site/2011/11/07/heterotopia-the-soul-of-ruins-in-vincent-j-stoker/

80 Nathan Jurgenson and PJ Rey, "Ambient Documentation: To Be is To See and To See is To Be", *Cyborgology,* 21 November 2011 http://thesocietypages.org/cyborgology/2011/11/21/ambient-documentation-to-be-is-to-see-and-to-see-is-to-be/

81 Susan Sontag, *On Photography.* 1978. London: Allen Lane

82 Abi Sutherland, "As you are, once was I; as I am, you will be", *Making Light,* 15 January 2012 http://nielsenhayden.com/makinglight/archives/01346C.html

83 Bruce Sterling, "Atemporality for the Creative Artist", *Wired*, 25 February 2010 http://www.wired.com/2010/02/atemporality-for-the-creative-artist/

84 Sean Posey, "What Separates Ruin Porn from Important Documentary Photography?", *Rustwire*, 14 June 2011 http://rustwire.com/2011/06/14/what-separates-ruin-porn-from-important-rust-belt-documentary-photography/

85 Matthew Christopher, "Confessions of a Ruin Pornographer: A Lurid Tale of Art, Double Standards, and Decay", 14 January 2012 http://www.abandonedamerica.us/life-as-a-ruin-pornographer

86 Ina Fried, "Intel Sociologist Says the Love Affair Between Us and Our Gadgets Is Turning Into a Real Relationship", *All Things D*, 12 September 2013 http://allthingsd.com/20130912/intel-sociologist-says-the-love-affair-between-us-and-our-gadgets-is-turning-into-a-real-relationship/

87 Sunny Moraine, "I Tell Thee All, I Can No More", *Clarkesworld*, No. 82, July 2013 http://clarkesworldmagazine.com/moraine_07_13/

88 Sarah Wanenchak, "All Watched Over by Machines of Loving Grace", *Cyborgology*, 15 October 2013 http://thesocietypages.org/cyborgology/2013/10/15/all-watched-over-by-machines-of-loving-grace/

89 Robin James, "Drones, Sound, and Super-Panoptic Surveillance", *Cyborgology*, 26 October 2013 http://thesocietypages.org/cyborgology/2013/10/26/drones-sound-and-super-panoptic-surveillance/

90 Jenny Davis, "Siri: Intersections of Gender, Economy, and Technology", *Cyborgology*, 24 October 2011 http://thesocietypages.org/cyborgology/2011/10/24/siri-intersections-of-gender-economy-and-technology/

91 A.C. Wise, "The Last Survivor of the Great Sexbot Revolution", *Clarkesworld*, No. 78, March 2013 http://clarkesworldmagazine.com/wise_03_13/

92 Sarah Wanenchak", "AIs of the world unite!", *Cyborgology*, 13 September 2013 http://thesocietypages.org/cyborgology/2013/09/13/ais-of-the-world-unite/

93 Adam Rothstein, "How to Write Drone Fiction", *The State*, 20 January 2013 http://www.thestate.ae/how-to-write-drone-fiction/

94 Robin James, "A Few Thoughts on 'Drone Sexuality': pt. 1, race and cyborg sexuality", *Cyborgology*, 27 December 2013 http://thesocietypages.org/cyborgology/2013/12/27/a-few-thoughts-on-drone-sexuality-pt-1-race-cyborg-sexuality/

95 Robin James, "More on Drone Sexuality: Droning, Knowing, and Binaries", *Cyborgology*, 03 January 2014
http://thesocietypages.org/cyborgology/2014/01/03/droning-knowing-binaries/

96 Whitney Erin Boesel, "Death and Mediation", *Cyborgology*, 30 December 2013
http://thesocietypages.org/cyborgology/2013/12/30/death-and-mediation/

97   Elaine Scarry, *The Body in Pain: The Making and Unmaking of the World*. 1985. Oxford: Oxford University Press

98   Fred Clark, "Holy Saturday", 18 April 2014
http://www.patheos.com/blogs/slacktivist/2014/04/18/holy-saturday-3/

ABOUT THE AUTHOR

Sunny Moraine is an author of various flavors of speculative fiction; the flavor in question depends upon a complex conjunction of different variables, the exact nature of which they have yet to specify or untangle. Their work has appeared in *Clarkesworld, Strange Horizons, Shimmer, Lightspeed, Apex Magazine,* and multiple Year's Best collections, as well as the anthologies *We See a Different Frontier* and *Long Hidden: Speculative Fiction from the Margins of History.* They are responsible for the novels *Line and Orbit* (cowritten with Lisa Soem), and *Labyrinthian,* as well as the Casting the Bones trilogy.

In additional to occasional authoring, Sunny is a doctoral candidate in sociology and a sometimes college instructor; that last may or may not have been a good move on the part of their department. Their academic alter-ego blogs weekly at *Cyborgology,* concerning technology and politics and fiction and reality and lots of other things. They unfortunately live just outside Washington DC in a creepy house with two cats and a very long-suffering husband.

www.ingramcontent.com/pod-product-compliance
Lightning Source LLC
Chambersburg PA
CBHW070105290526
45789CB00005B/1928